Praise for *How to Personalize Learning*

"Many teachers are familiar with UDL, and they may want to try it in their classrooms, but they just don't know how to get started. With this book, educators don't just learn about UDL, they do UDL as they complete a number of activities designed to get them thinking about their most deeply held beliefs about learning and ease them into a new role as the 'lead learner' in their classrooms."

—**Luis Pérez**
Inclusive Learning Consultant
Independent Consultant
St. Petersburg, Florida

"This book provides teachers with a tool to refocus and keep their best practices while helping them to identify those areas of instruction where shifts need to occur, and the 'how to' to make it happen! So inspiring, engaging, and motivational—and the companion website for technology and sharing is awesome! *How to Personalize Learning* is a user's guide designed by experts who personally and professionally relate; Bray and McClaskey simply 'Get it.'

—**Diana Petschauer**
Assistive Technology Professional, CEO
Assistive Technology for Education & Access4Employment
Wolfeboro Falls, New Hampshire

"Bray and McClaskey are arguably the foremost champions for personalizing learning. *How to Personalize Learning: A Practical Guide for Getting Started and Going Deeper* will be the compendium to personalize learning and a guiding light for educators as they navigate their journey with their learners to personalize learning. The tools, rich examples, and insights included in the book will be instrumental in the transformation of students into learners."

—**Pam Lowe**
Author: Missouri Then & Now: Activity Book; University of Missouri Press
Educator and Education Consultant/Coach

"As the title suggests, Kathleen and Barbara have prepared some really solid, practical 'how to' guidelines for educators looking to understand and achieve the promise of personalizing learning."

—*Steve Nordmark*
Chief Academic Officer, Knovation, Inc.
Cincinnati, Ohio

"This book will provide you and your team the steps toward personalizing learning for your students. It involves your input throughout with activities that are built around personalized learning principles."

—*Kevin McLaughlin,*
Deputy Head Teacher, Farndon Fields Primary School
Leicester, United Kingdom

"Your learning journey about creating personalized learning environments just became so much easier! Bray and McClaskey's practical guide provides a clear and well signposted path forward to transforming any learner's journey. I found the book highly readable, incredibly practical, and full of useful strategies to move educators from just discussing ideas about personalized learning to actively implementing and growing a personalized learning culture. It really is THE Rosetta Stone of personalized learning. No other resource so deftly distills the WHAT and the WHY with the HOW TO of personalized learning."

—*Greg Alchin*
Inclusive Design Consultant, Alchin Consulting
Orange, New South Wales, Australia

"This guide provides actionable steps for all educators, from the busy main office to the crowded classroom, to develop the culture, expertise, and strategies needed for truly personalized learning. Once implementation is rolling out, Bray and McClaskey provide guidance for professional reflection and growth along the way. Personalization provides benefits to all stakeholders, and this book helps all stakeholders understand their roles and how they will grow through the experience."

—*Kerry Gallagher*
Digital Learning Specialist, St. John's Prep
Director of K–12 Education, ConnectSafely.org
Haverhill, Massachusetts

"This book is a transformative treatise for all levels on catalyzing enhanced efficacy—from community culture to the classroom learner—so that personalized learning becomes a reality in even the most traditional classrooms. Whether you are the community member who dares to think differently or the classroom teacher that knows deep down that something just isn't working, *How to Personalize Learning: A Practical Guide for Getting Started and Going Deeper* is the seminal book to get you started on your personalized learning journey."

—*Patrick Riley*
Cognitive Coach, Green River Regional Educational Cooperative
kid-FRIENDLy, Race to the Top-District Grant
Kentucky

"*How to Personalize Learning* is the book every school needs their teachers to read. The authors take teachers on an enlightening journey where they reflect on how they uniquely learn. This book also is a guide with practical ideas and many resources to help teachers make learning accessible and engaging to all students. This book is for the teacher with the big heart who wants to ensure all students leave wanting to continue their learning journeys."

—*Shelly Sanchez Terrell*
Teacher, International Speaker, and
Author of The 30 Goals Challenge for Teachers*,*
http://www.shellyterrell.com/

"Bray and McClaskey have done it again! This book provides such essential explanations and tools that any person reading it should be able to immediately construct their personalized instruction and learning environment. The multiple options for activities help teachers apply their personal preferences to more deeply connect with this work. This book even further demonstrates how important it is to make learning personal."

—*Kecia Ray, EdD*
Executive Director, Center for Digital Education
Nashville, Tennessee

"Bray and McClaskey designed this book with teachers in mind. As with *Make Learning Personal*, the book is a treasure trove of resources, studies, and sound practices. Don't go it alone—buy copies for your personal learning community and enjoy the conversations. This is a must-have if your school is moving to competency based education and blended learning."

—*Andy Littlefield*
Co-Director of Technology
Online Educator
Exeter Region Cooperative School District, New Hampshire

"*How to Personalize Learning: A Practical Guide for Getting Started and Going Deeper* is a rich resource for any in-service or pre-service teacher, school or district administrator, special educator, or parent. In my more than 25 years of working with teachers and with school administrators, what

I most appreciate about this guide are the numerous case studies and tangible examples of how the practices work in the real world."

—*Dr. Cynthia Sistek-Chandler*
Associate Professor
Teacher Education, Sanford College of Education
National University, California

"In this compact and powerful book, Barbara Bray and Kathleen McClaskey offer teaching teams, school leadership groups, and whole faculties a way to engage learners in managing their own learning. *How to Personalize Learning* creates a comprehensive process for managing a long and complex process, preparing all learners to assess themselves, build skills, work toward personal and academic goals, and build the skills and knowledge that help them move toward their goals. This is a highly practical book that forms a reliable foundation for empowering a school community striving to make our schools work for all learners."

—*John H. Clarke*
Professor Emeritus, University of Vermont
Author of Personalized Learning: Student-designed
Pathways to High School Graduation

"Barbara Bray and Kathleen McClaskey are leaders in how to personalize learning. *How to Personalize Learning: A Practical Guide for Getting Started and Going Deeper* breaks down personalizing learning in a way that not only makes good sense, but it makes it easy for educators to do what they know is right for their learners. This guide will help classrooms come alive with engaged, excited learners whose learning will not only meet, but go beyond standards. The many examples of successful personalized learning cultures will inspire and shape the future of teaching and learning."

—*Linda K. Taber Ullah, MA, MEd*
Coach, Personalize Learning, LLC
Instructor, Krause Center for Innovation
Foothill College, Washington

"*How to Personalize Learning* is a valuable guide for educators at all levels of knowledge around personalizing learning, PBL, and UDL. A new teacher can use it like a 'how to' manual to go step-by-step through the book, promoting learner voice and choice while developing engaging lessons and projects. Seasoned, 'master' teachers will benefit from the usable Tables and 'Conversation Starters' which can act as cues to remind every teacher that they are learners first, that best practice is still practice, and that our practice can always be improved."

—*David Truss*
Lead Administrator, Inquiry Hub Secondary School
Vice Principal, Coquitlam Open Learning, SD43
Coquitlam, Canada

"Barbara Bray and Kathleen McClaskey continue to demonstrate how they are two of the leading ladies of personalized learning with their practical and positive portrayal of a learner-centered approach to education. They have captured the essence of next practices over best practices by providing a timely 'how-to' manual for preparing community, college, and career-ready learners who understand they are in charge of their own learning. *How to Personalize Learning* is the perfect read for an individual educator or team of educators whose goal is to prepare learners who will take control of their own learning as preparation for taking control of their own life as an adult.

—*Bryan Bronn, Principal*
Branson Junior High
Branson, Missouri

"In *How to Personalize Learning*, Bray and McClaskey provide sound, practical approaches to meet the needs and interests of each learner at a time in education where personalization and customization of instruction is a critical, core tenet of learning. Their solid pedagogical foundation and sound teaching strategies can help every educator help prepare learners for the living, learning, working, and growing challenges they will experience in their lifetimes. I strongly recommend this book to educators everywhere making the shift in their professional practice."

—*Walter McKenzie*
The One and Only Surfaquarium
Washington, D.C.

"For educators and learning communities that are ready to dive deep into transforming their learning expectations and environments, this book is an essential resource. The combination of field experiences and models, vetted resources to make learning active rather than passive, and the structures provided to support personalizing learning in any learning experience, makes the resource so important. Educators can rely on the information from these rock stars of personalized learning, knowing that it is as current as it can be, as it provides contacts and resources to follow-up with, and moves the theory of personalizing learning into practice. "

—*Caroline Patrie*
Innovation Coach
Addison North East Supervisory Union
Bristol, Vermont

"Educators must change their perspectives of both teaching and learning to be in a position to grow citizens prepared to thrive and excel in our changing world. This practical guide lays out the foundation for both leadership and classroom practitioners to begin this journey by understanding the changing landscape and providing practical applications of personalized learning pedagogy."

—*Cynthia Dunlap, MEd*
Educational Technology Consultant
Nashua, New Hampshire

"Bray and McClaskey have already inspired us to *Make Learning Personal*, but now they have given us some points of entry that we can start with tomorrow in *How to Personalize Learning: A Practical Guide for Getting Started and Going Deeper*. Now we have an important next step for teachers wanting to put learning back into the hands of the learner."

—*John Parker*
Chief Technology Innovation Officer
Cherokee County Schools, North Carolina

"Grounded in a shared vision and beliefs, Bray and McClaskey provide practical steps to guide teachers through the process of discovering the unique learner in every child. Furthermore, the reader is coached on how to personalize for an entire class, with practical advice, activities, and hands-on tools. This is more than just the typical 'education needs to change' book. This is a practical guide for teachers to actually make changes to positively transform education as learners become owners of their own learning."

—*Jon Tanner*
Director of Technology and Personalized Learning
Oregon School District, Wisconsin

"Bray and McClaskey's first book, *Make Learning Personal*, does an outstanding job of defining personalized learning, developing common language, and making a strong case for WHY this is good for our learners. This book is the perfect companion as it serves as a practical guide that moves educators from the abstract to the concrete, delving into the HOW to personalize learning."

—*Betty Wottreng*
Director of Technology Services
Verona Area School District, Wisconsin

How to Personalize Learning

How to Personalize Learning

A Practical Guide for Getting Started and Going Deeper

Barbara Bray | Kathleen McClaskey

CORWIN
A SAGE Publishing Company

FOR INFORMATION:

Corwin

A SAGE Company

2455 Teller Road

Thousand Oaks, California 91320

(800) 233-9936

www.corwin.com

SAGE Publications Ltd.

1 Oliver's Yard

55 City Road

London EC1Y 1SP

United Kingdom

SAGE Publications India Pvt. Ltd.

B 1/I 1 Mohan Cooperative Industrial Area

Mathura Road, New Delhi 110 044

India

SAGE Publications Asia-Pacific Pte. Ltd.

3 Church Street

#10-04 Samsung Hub

Singapore 049483

ISBN: 9781506338538

Acquisitions Editor: Ariel Bartlett

Senior Associate Editor: Desirée A. Bartlett

Senior Editorial Assistant: Andrew Olson

Copy Editor: Robin Gold

Typesetter: C&M Digitals (P) Ltd.

Proofreader: Dennis W. Webb

Cover Designer: Anupama Krishnan

Marketing Manager: Jill Margulies

16 17 18 19 20 10 9 8 7 6 5 4 3 2 1

Contents

Foreword

Dr. David Rose, one of the originators of Universal Design for Learning, often says that "teaching is emotional work." By that I take him to mean that teaching is not just a purely technocratic endeavor. It is more than just delivering the right content at the right time, though that is important for sure. It is also more than just assessing how well students have mastered said content, though again that is important as well. Rather, at the heart of teaching are the relationships we remember from our best learning experiences. If you were to close your eyes right now and think back to a time when you were most engaged with learning, you will probably see a teacher who was invested in your success, who encouraged you and helped you gain confidence in your abilities, and who balanced the right mix of support with freedom and trust. In short, you were in the presence of someone who, perhaps without realizing it, already understood what it means to be an expert learner, one who driven by his or her passion can then take ownership of learning and do the hard work that is needed for success. What if you could be that teacher for every learner who walks into your classroom?

Helping all of our learners develop their learning expertise is the focus of this book. It is also the ultimate goal of Universal Design for Learning, the framework the authors have chosen to frame their discussion of learning. Notice that I am using the term *learners* instead of *students*. This change in my thinking and vocabulary has been influenced by my reading of Barbara and Kathleen's work. As they state, students are passive recipients of content and have little choice in how they participate in education. Learners are empowered, and as a result take on a more active role in the design of their education. If as some people suggest, language shapes our actions, then right away with Chapter 1 of this book you will be on your way to reshaping your teaching practice. Starting with the language you use, you will be challenged to rethink the traditional teacher-student role in order to close the emotional distance it creates and develop a more equitable relationship with your learners. Thus, right from the start of this book, you will be engaged in the "emotional work" of teaching as you seek to build a different kind of learning environment, one where strong relationships based on trust and shared responsibility are the norm.

With a common language, vision, and understanding of what personalization really means as a strong foundation, the rest of the book seeks to translate the latest research about learning into actionable strategies you can immediately implement in your classroom. In this way, the more abstract concept of "the learner" is translated into the more concrete one of "your learners." This is accomplished through a number of activities (creating a Learner Profile and a Personal Learning Plan as just two examples) that help you get to know who your learners really are, what drives and motivates them, and what they need to do their best work and reach their full potential. I have a feeling that as you help your learners with their Learner Profiles, Personal Learning Backpacks, and Personal Learning Plans you yourself will rediscover who you are as a learner. In doing so, you will also rediscover your own passion for teaching and the values that caused you to go into this profession in the first place. At the end of the book, you will be asked to create a 60-second pitch that will serve as a reminder of your core values and hopefully become your compass as you seek to align your practice with those values.

While I agree with Dr. Rose that "teaching is emotional work," I would add that it is also "civic work." As educators, we can play a role in ensuring that everyone can enjoy life in a fair and equitable society, but only to the extent that we dedicate ourselves to developing citizens who are actively engaged in the life of their communities. This requires a commitment to providing all citizens with the skills they will need to be active participants in conversations about the future, including the ability to be critical thinkers and to appreciate and value diversity. We can do this work in each one of our classrooms as we develop each learner's agency and ability to live a self-determined life, which is a major focus of this book starting in Chapter 3.

One of my favorite quotes, attributed to former House Speaker Tip O'Neill, is that "all politics is local." Similarly, all "learning is local" in the sense that it is not removed from the life of the community where a school is located and the issues that impact the lives of individual learners. In this way, learning is once again more than a technocratic exercise of delivering content and information. It is also about helping learners make connections: not only connections between the topics and ideas discussed in the classroom, but more importantly between those topics and ideas and the learners themselves. This is what "deeper learning" as discussed in Chapter 8 is all about: going beyond the surface, and isolated facts that have little relevance to learners, to focus on the big ideas that move and inspire them to be the innovative thinkers and agents for change we will need to solve the complex problems of our shared future.

If you have picked up this book, you probably agree with me that the technocratic approach to education has not worked, and you are looking for a new direction. If that is the case, then I invite you to not just read this book, but use it as a blueprint for rethinking every aspect of your approach to teaching, from the questions that guide your lessons to the tools you use to engage learners and make education more accessible to them. This book asks a lot of you, but it gives you even more in return. By that I mean that it asks you to consider some of the tough questions that are often glossed over in most education books: what does it mean to be a teacher, and more importantly, what does it mean to be a learner? However, as you ask those tough questions, you will also be provided with the tools you need to formulate some good responses and take meaningful action. The many activities and resources found in each chapter will be an invaluable resource as you rethink your role and begin to engage in the "emotional" and "civic" work of teaching needed to create a better society for future generations.

Luis Pérez, Inclusive Learning Consultant
Independent Consultant
St. Petersburg, Florida

Acknowledgments

This practical guide was initiated by educators around the world who asked us over the last 2 years how to personalize learning in their schools. They wanted information about how to create new learning environments where all learners have the opportunity to own their learning, have a voice and choice in their learning, and become prepared to enter a world where jobs are yet to be imagined. These requests are why we decided to write this book. We want to thank every administrator, teacher, learner, colleague, and friend who encouraged us to bring this practical guide to fruition.

We could not have written this book without the support of close colleagues and educators. We would like to give special thanks to Diana Petschauer from Assistive Technology for Education who offered hours of invaluable advice on the Learner Profile, Personal Learning Backpack, and Personal Learning Plan in Chapter 4. We want to thank Dr. James Rickabaugh and Jean Garrity, directors of the Institute for Personalized Learning, for working with us on the collaborative blog series on learner agency that helped us take the next step to define each of the elements we detail in Chapter 3. We owe Sylvia Duckworth a big thank you for turning each of the elements into delightful and engaging images that tell a story about how learning changes as learners progress from teacher-centered to learner-driven environments.

We would like to thank Dr. David Rose and Anne Meyer from the Center for Applied Special Technology (CAST), who introduced the educational world to Universal Design for Learning (UDL) and who continue to share and expand their research on learning and the variability of learners. We want to mention and give thanks to Kathleen Cushman at What Kids Can Do (WKCD) for her research and book *The Motivation Equation* (2013) about understanding what motivates kids to learn. We want to thank Rebecca Wolfe and the Students at the Center Hub for sharing a plethora of key resources and research to help schools create learner-centered environments. We also want to thank the Jobs of the Future and Council of State School Officers (CCSSO) for the Educator Competencies for Personalized, Learning-Centered Teaching that guides educators to develop the skills they will need to create learner-centered environments. We have a special thank you to Chris Watkins, a reader and researcher at the University of London, who continues to inspire our work. Chris shares in his writings how to make sense of learning, the importance of learners driving their own learning, and what type of learning environments need to be created for all learners.

We would like to acknowledge our colleagues, Cyndi Dunlap, David Truss, Jon Tanner, Steve Nordmark, and Andy Littlefield, who reviewed the first draft of this book, critiqued it, and offered their invaluable advice and feedback on how to make it better.

This book is filled with inspiring stories from educators who we owe our heartfelt gratitude for sharing their vision, beliefs, and experiences as they transformed classrooms, schools, and school districts into learner-centered environments.

- Virgel Hammonds is chief learning officer at KnowledgeWorks and former superintendent at Regional School Unit Two (RSU 2) in Maine who shares how the district pulled all stakeholders together around a vision and shared beliefs.
- Dr. Michelle Schmitz, principal, and Susan Maynor, blended learning coach, at EPiC Elementary in Missouri, share their story of how they developed a set of beliefs that were established with everyone in their school community.
- Bill McGrath, instructional specialist at Montgomery County Public Schools in Maryland (MCPS), advocates for the use of Universal Design for Learning in MCPS and what it means for teachers to develop expert learners.
- Dr. James Rickabaugh, director of the Institute for Personalized Learning in Wisconsin, explains that many factors and experiences can undermine the strength of self-efficacy and why it is the secret sauce for learner agency.
- The Liberty Elementary School Personalized Learning Team from Riverside, California, share how team members adapted the Learner Profile that started the conversations allowing teachers to get to know each learner as learners create their Personalized Learning Plans.
- Caroline Patrie, a long-time personalized learning coordinator for Mount Abraham Union Middle/High School and currently Addison Northeast Supervisory Union (ANESU) innovation coach, shared the history of their Personal Learning Plans.
- Starr Sackstein, high school English and journalism teacher at World Journalism Preparatory School in New York and author of *Power of Questioning* (2016), shares why it is important to put the power of questions in learners' hands.

- Jackie Gerstein, EdD, who teaches online courses in educational technology for Boise State, American Intercontinental, and Western Governors University, shares how you can make a lesson or project relevant and apply new learning in meaningful context.
- Paula Ford, a kindergarten teacher in California, shares the story about a project with a school in Africa to show that even young learners are up to tackling challenges, can use inquiry, and can be creative and innovative.
- Pernille Ripp, seventh-grade teacher in the Oregon School District in Wisconsin, reflects about transforming the culture of learning in her classroom to help learners discover their superpowers and provides suggestions for teachers how to make learning visible.
- Rich Czyz, director of curriculum and instruction at Stafford Township School District, and Trevor Bryan, a K–5 art teacher in New Jersey, who are co-founders of the Four O-Clock Faculty blog, provide tips and tricks for educators on culture.
- Patrick Riley, cognitive coach, Green River Regional Educational Cooperative, kid·FRIENDLy, Race to the Top-District Grant in Kentucky, walks through his coaching journey about what it is like to grow a culture of learning in classrooms.

Thank you to the educators around the world who have shared your stories with us. Your deep reflections and understanding of what personalized learning means to you and your learners continues to fuel our passion and expand our thinking about personalized learning. A special thank you to our team: Linda Ullah, coach and mentor, and Pam Lowe, coach and marketing associate, who are dedicated in making a difference for teachers and learners and have been invaluable in helping us make learning personal.

We definitely want to thank our husbands, Tom Bray and Jim McClaskey, who generously give their daily support in so many different ways so we can pursue our mission. We want to thank our wonderful children, Sara Zimmerman and Andrew Bray (Barbara's children), and Joshua McClaskey and Seth McClaskey (Kathleen's children) and our grandchildren, who inspire us every day to work endless hours to make this a world where all learners can follow their passions and realize their hopes and dreams.

PUBLISHER'S ACKNOWLEDGMENTS

Corwin gratefully acknowledges the contributions of the following reviewers:

Greg Alchin
Inclusive Design Consultant
Alchin Consulting
Calare, NSW, Australia

Chris Henderson
Principal
Knox County Schools
Knoxville, TN

About the Authors

Barbara Bray and Kathleen McClaskey are co-founders of Personalize Learning, LLC (www.personalizelearning.com) and co-authors of *Make Learning Personal*.

 **Barbara Bray** is a writer, speaker, instructional designer, and creative learning strategist who enjoys connecting people and ideas relating to transforming education. She has focused on creating learner-centered environments for over 25 years and coined the term *Making Learning Personal* in 2000 because she believed that education really needed to be all about our learners and learning first. In addition to focusing on personalizing learning, Barbara posts on Rethinking Learning (barbarabray.net) and is the founder/owner of My eCoach (my-ecoach.com). My eCoach is based on a coaching platform for teachers because they are learners too and need ongoing support as they change teaching practice. She wrote the professional development column for CUE for 17 years and received the CUE Gold and Platinum disks for her contributions to educational technology for the advancement of teaching and learning.

Barbara is passionate about writing, sharing stories of transforming learning, and facilitating change. She is encouraged when she sees teachers and administrators immersing themselves in challenges that stretch their minds and imagination. She loves combining the neuroscience of learning with the design-thinking process and project-based learning in a learner-centered environment. Barbara helps schools and organizations develop sustainable coaching programs, design professional learning to transform teaching practice, and guide the redesign of flexible learning spaces. She enjoys working with leadership teams in guiding change so all stakeholders are committed to a shared vision around teaching and learning.

Barbara lives in the San Francisco Bay Area with her best friend and husband Tom, whom she has been married to for 46 years. She is grateful for her sisters Sandy Ritz, Terry Leach, and Janet Ritz for their ongoing support over the years. Barbara feels so lucky to watch how her two creative children, Sara Zimmerman and Andrew Bray, are passionate about what they do and how they live and for her amazing granddaughter, Cali, who constantly shares what she has learned and created on her own. Barbara wants to thank her friends and family who inspire her to follow her purpose to make learning personal for all learners.

Kathleen McClaskey has been on a mission the last three decades to level the playing field for all learners and to assist educators in discovering the learner in every child. In her career, she has been a middle school teacher, K–12 administrator, professional developer, innovative leader, author, and futurist who believes that everyone on the planet is a learner. As an educational technologist for over 33 years, graduate instructor in Massachusetts and New Hampshire and a Universal Design for Learning consultant, she has worked worldwide in training thousands of teachers in using tools to instruct all learners in the classroom. She most recently had the opportunity to go to Dubai to keynote and train teachers in the Middle East on personalized learning. Over the last 15 years, Kathleen directed and designed the professional development using Universal Design for Learning as the framework in multiple technology-based projects in math, science, literacy, and autism to build 21st century classrooms and sustainable learner-centered environments. She is passionate in empowering learners with tools, skills, and learning strategies so that they can become independent learners with agency who can realize their hopes and dreams and have choices in college, career, and life.

Kathleen is co-founder and chief executive officer of Personalize Learning, LLC, founder/owner of EdTech Associates, Inc., and the president and advocacy chairperson for the New Hampshire Society for Technology in Education (NHSTE), an affiliate of International Society for Technology in Education (ISTE). Her advocacy work has spanned more than 10 years where she has advocated in Congress for legislation and funding for educational technology during that time. In 2012, she was recognized for her advocacy work with the ISTE Public Policy Advocate of the Year Award.

Kathleen lives in New Hampshire with her husband and best friend, Jim, who she has been married to for 43 years. She has two wonderful sons, Joshua and Seth, and two handsome grandsons, Austyn and Benny, who all continue to serve as her daily inspiration to personalize learning for every learner. She is thankful to have family, friends, and colleagues that have supported her lifelong mission to level the playing field for all learners.

Introduction

You entered the field of education to make a difference. You believe that each child is unique in his or her own way. Yet, you only know what you were taught as a learner in school and in your teacher education or graduate program: to be the expert providing all the content in a "one size fits all" manner. Because of the structure of "traditional school," teachers tend to be the ones responsible and held accountable for what learners learn. If learners are not the ones accountable, they are not motivated to learn. Isn't this backwards? Personalized learning helps learners become intrinsically motivated to learn, so they own and drive their learning. You will notice we intentionally use the word *learners* instead of *students*. A *student* refers to someone who is being taught in a school or an educational institution. A *learner* knows how he or she learns best and takes responsibility for her or his learning. We only keep the word *student* when a contributor includes that in our book.

You may already have an understanding of personalized learning and the major concepts for changing teacher and learner roles. However, you may not know how to put it into practice in your class or school. If you are reading this book, you are ready to transform teaching and how learners learn. You want your learners to take responsibility for their learning and become self-directed, independent learners. You believe that to prepare kids for their future, you have to change how you teach and what school looks like. You know you are a learner, too. You have been looking for the tools and strategies to support transforming your classroom and your role as a teacher. You will find that this is your practical guide to help you on your journey.

> Personalized learning helps learners become intrinsically motivated to learn, so they own and drive their learning to become self-directed, independent learners.

THE PURPOSE OF THIS PRACTICAL GUIDE

We designed this book to provide you the first steps to transform teaching practice and to explore what it means for learners today to be prepared for college, career, and life. We do know that some educators are past the first steps in transforming teaching practice so we included sections to go deeper. This practical guide provides strategies, tips, activities, and resources to help you launch and expand personalized learning in your classroom and school. After we wrote our book *Make Learning Personal* teachers and administrators from all over the world were telling us the same message: that they see an urgency to change school and how they teach because kids are different today and will need different skills to be prepared for their future. If you are starting with this book on the how, you may want to read and refer to *Make Learning Personal*, which covers the what, who, wow, where, and why of personalized learning.

We heard loud and clear from teachers that there is a critical disconnect between traditional teaching and what kids need so learning becomes meaningful. There has to be a purpose that is relevant to the real world and their lives. We understand that each educator has different situations, experiences, and perspectives, so we designed this book to meet the needs of teachers in different roles with multiple examples and suggestions. Throughout the book, we also offer suggestions for administrators and parents to help change teaching and learning across the school community.

HOW TO USE THIS PRACTICAL GUIDE

Because this book is about personalized learning, we wanted to make sure we integrated multiple options for the activities. Our Companion Website includes digital versions that complement the activities and resources in each chapter.

The Book: *As you read and review the book, you will see we added common features in all chapters.*

- **Overview**: Each chapter starts with an overview that begins with a big question and provides definitions and takeaways and may include what you need for background information or summaries of what was included in our book, *Make Learning Personal*.
- **Activities**: Each chapter has topics that may include activities with directions and links to resources and digital versions of the activities.
- **Audience**: Activities will be identified with an icon for group or individual activities.

- **Conversation Starters:** Each activity or group of activities will end with questions or prompts to expand conversations in the book and on the Companion Website.
- **Examples and Models:** Educators, schools, or districts provide their own stories, examples, models, and strategies around topics.
- **Extending Thinking:** Multiple sidebars and pull quotes will encourage you to reflect and extend your thinking with ideas and questions.

- **Digital Version:** The Companion Website logo indicates downloadable resources and activities.
- **QR Codes:** Scan the QR Codes to link to websites that extend the topic.

- **Build the Common Language:** At the end of each chapter, there will be prompts to add the common language relating to personalized learning.

- **Review, Learn, Apply:** At the end of each chapter there will be questions or prompts to help you reflect on your learning and how you will take action from what you learned.

Review: Stop and notice what you learned.

Learn: What new insights and understandings did you learn?

Apply: What future action is planned in light of your new understanding?

The Companion Website: *Created to extend the activities and provide downloadable resources.* The link to the website is http://bit.ly/howtopl and the passcode is in Chapter 8 and is the last word in the first paragraph.

- **Tabs:** Each chapter has its own tab with one or more pages.
- **Activities:** Under each chapter tab are separate pages for the activities with directions and links to downloadable files.
- **Book Reference:** We've added the page numbers to relevant sections in our first book, *Make Learning Personal*, for your reference.
- **Sharing Ideas:** The Companion Website has several places for you to share your ideas and reflections.
  - The **Build the Common Language** tab will include an interactive Padlet for you to start adding your voice to the common language.
  - **Conversation Starters:** At the bottom of a page in the Companion Website, you will be able to add your voice by leaving a comment or replying to someone else's comment.
  - The last chapter will provide a place for you to share your 60-second speech.

OVERVIEW OF THE BOOK AND WHAT TO EXPECT IN EACH CHAPTER

Chapter 1: Build a Common Language

In Chapter 1, you will take away an understanding of the differences between personalization, differentiation, and individualization; how relationships matter in building a culture of learning; and how a vision and shared beliefs support building the common language of personalized learning. Activities will center around the Personalization v. Differentiation v. Individualization (PDI) chart, adding your voice to the common language around personalized learning, brainstorming shared beliefs, and including prompts to consider when creating vision.

Chapter 2: How Learners Learn Best

Chapter 2 provides an overview of Universal Design for Learning (UDL) and how you use the UDL lens to understand how learners learn best. This chapter will provide an understanding of UDL as the lens to personalize learning; a foundation of the UDL Principles and Guidelines; how Access, Engage, and Express can be used to apply the UDL Principles in practice; and how to develop expert learners.

Chapter 3: Develop Learner Agency

In Chapter 3, we'll discuss how to develop agency so that learners become independent, self-directed, and self-motivated. Learner agency involves seven elements: voice, choice, engagement, motivation, ownership, purpose, and self-efficacy. Each element includes its own continuum that learners and teachers can refer to as they move to agency. We include charts and graphics for each continuum and show how learners move along each continuum from teacher-centered to learner-centered to learner-driven.

Chapter 4: Discover the Learner in Every Child

Chapter 4 introduces three helpful tools: the Learner Profile, Personal Learning Backpack, and Personal Learning Plan. The Learner Profile, which includes Who I Am as a Learner, helps learners understand how they learn best. The Personal Learning Backpack includes a template and guide to collect resources and strategies to support how the learner learns. The Personal Learning Plan builds on the Profile and Backpack to help the learner identify strengths and challenges the learner has and then set goals and action steps to develop the skills to overcome these challenges and enhance her or his strengths. Learners will be able to identify how they will meet and monitor their learning goals.

Chapter 5: Personalize Learning for a Whole Class

Chapter 5 provides instructions, templates, and strategies for the teacher to anticipate four learners at the ends of the learning spectrum to develop a Class Learning Snapshot. Teachers can then use the template for the Class Learning Toolkit, which includes the tools, apps, resources, and instructional methods to engage the maximum number of learners in the class. This becomes a tool for teachers to universally design instruction, which will be covered in Chapter 7.

Chapter 6: Lesson Design With All Learners in Mind

Chapter 6 helps reduce barriers to the curriculum by maximizing the learning for all learners using the UDL lens of Access, Engage, and Express. We offer examples of strategies teachers can use to encourage voice and choice in lessons and activities in a Stage One Personalized Learning Environment. This chapter includes an understanding of the UDL Lesson Review Process by applying it to one's own lesson, knowing how to create a vocabulary activity with visuals, and designing a lesson with all learners in mind.

Chapter 7: Delve Into Deeper Learning

Chapter 7 will show how to help learners exercise their agency to go deeper into their learning. We'll cover strategies to encourage learners to develop driving questions around a theme or concept, know the difference between projects and project-based learning (PBL), determine key understandings and standards, and create PBL activities that include a pitch, reflection, and description of how learners demonstrate evidence of learning as they learn.

Chapter 8: Learner Agency Across the Stages

The Stages of Personalized Learning Environments (PLE) was developed to provide a process for teachers who want to create learner-centered and eventually learner-driven environments. Stage One PLE is teacher-centered. Stage Two PLE is learner-centered. Stage Three PLE is learner-driven. We recently revised the Stages of PLE to version 5 and combined the seven elements of learner agency listed in Chapter 3 as a crosswalk so teachers can understand what personalized learning looks like at each stage.

Chapter 9: Create a Culture of Learning

Personalized learning environments cannot thrive without the right school culture. This chapter will include how to build a culture that cares about everyone, to understand the relationships between personal needs and school practice, to talk about personalizing learning with your learners and colleagues, and to develop a learning environment in your classroom that invites voice, choice, and engagement. The culminating activities include Connect the Dots and creating a 60-second speech on the rationale to personalize learning.

We designed this book to provide examples, models, practical strategies, and activities for personalizing learning for teachers, administrators, parents, and learners of all ages. We hope you enjoy this book as your guide to help you along your journey.

1

Build a
Common Language

Why is it necessary to have a common language
around personalized learning?

Personalized learning is a culture shift. It is about transforming teaching and learning. To move a school or district to personalized learning environments, all stakeholders need to have a common language and understanding of personalized learning in conversations inside and outside school. In this chapter, you will take away an understanding of the differences between personalization, differentiation, and individualization, that focus needs to be about the learner, and of how a vision and shared belief system support building the common language around personalized learning.

DEFINE PERSONALIZED LEARNING

Personalized learning starts with the learner. The teacher is the guide for the learners on their personal journeys. When learners have choices to interact with the content and discuss what they watched, read, and learned, they are actively participating in learning. Encouraging learner voice and choice is the key difference of differentiation and individualization. When learners have a voice in how they learn and a choice in how they engage with content and express what they know, they are more motivated to want to learn and own their learning.

The Personalization vs. Differentiation vs. Individualization (PDI) chart (Figure 1.1) was created to clarify the differences in these terms. In 2010, the National Educational Technology Plan defined these three as they related to instruction and implied that personalization is teacher-centered. We needed to emphasize the differences: *Differentiation* and *individualization* are teacher-centered. *Personalization* is learner-centered. We included a link to the PDI (v3) chart on the Companion Website.

| Figure 1.1 | PDI Chart (v3) |

Personalization vs. Differentiation vs. Individualization Chart (v3)		
Personalization	**Differentiation**	**Individualization**
The Learner . . .	*The Teacher . . .*	*The Teacher . . .*
drives their own learning.	provides instruction to groups of learners.	provides instruction to an individual learner.
connects learning with interests, talents, passions, and aspirations.	adjusts learning needs for groups of learners.	accommodates learning needs for the individual learner.
actively participates in the design of their learning.	designs instruction based on the learning needs of different groups of learners.	customizes instruction based on the learning needs of the individual learner.
owns and is responsible for their learning that includes their voice and choice on how and what they learn.	is responsible for a variety of instruction for different groups of learners.	is responsible for modifying instruction based on the needs of the individual learner.
identifies goals for their learning plan and benchmarks as they progress along their learning path with guidance from teacher.	identifies the same objectives for different groups of learners as they do for the whole class.	identifies the same objectives for all learners with specific objectives for individuals who receive one-on-one support.
acquires the skills to select and use the appropriate technology and resources to support and enhance their learning.	selects technology and resources to support the learning needs of different groups of learners.	selects technology and resources to support the learning needs of the individual learner.
builds a network of peers, experts, and teachers to guide and support their learning.	supports groups of learners who are reliant on them for their learning.	understands the individual learner is dependent on them to support their learning.
demonstrates mastery of content in a competency-based system.	monitors learning based on Carnegie unit (seat time) and grade level.	monitors learning based on Carnegie unit (seat time) and grade level.
becomes a self-directed, expert learner who monitors progress and reflects on learning based on mastery of content and skills.	uses data and assessments to modify instruction for groups of learners and provides feedback to individual learners to advance learning.	uses data and assessments to measure progress of what the individual learner learned and did not learn to decide next steps in their learning.

Assessment AS and FOR Learning with minimal OF Learning	Assessment OF and FOR Learning	Assessment OF Learning
Personalization vs. Differentiation vs. Individualization Chart (v3), (2013) by Barbara Bray & Kathleen McClaskey is licensed under a Creative Commons Attribution- NonCommercial-NoDerivs 3.0 Unported License.		

Source: Personalize Learning, LLC.

ACTIVITY 1.1
PDI Empty Cells

After we created the PDI chart, educators asked us how to use the chart to help build the common language in their districts. Sandra Baker, Associate Executive Director of Green River Regional Educational Cooperative and Project Director of kid-FRIENDLy in Bowling Green, Kentucky, came up with an idea to build deeper conversations around the PDI chart that she shared with us: The PDI Empty Cells Activity.

The PDI Empty Cells Activity

This is a group activity for teachers, administrators, and other stakeholders to build an understanding of the differences between personalization, differentiation, and individualization:

- Before you hand out the PDI chart, you will be distributing the PDI Empty Cells Chart (Figure 1.2) along with a set of descriptor cards for the cells to each group.
- Each group can work in pairs or with three to four people who will work together to guess what traits go in each column.
- The PDI Empty Cells Activity and the PDI Descriptor Cards (Figure 1.3) are available to download from the Companion Website. *[FYI: The link and passcode information is in the Introduction.]*

Directions

1. Print enough copies of the PDI Empty Cells Chart so each group has one copy.

2. Print a copy of the PDI Descriptor Cards on 8.5 x 11 pages for each group.

3. Cut out the PDI descriptor cards and place them into an envelope.

4. Provide a copy of the PDI Empty Cells Chart and an envelope with the PDI Descriptor Cards to each group.

5. Have each group place the descriptor cards in the cells under each column in the chart.

6. Go to "Conversation Starters" to drive the discussions around the chart.

Figure 1.2 PDI Empty Cells Chart

Personalization	Differentiation	Individualization
The Learner...	The Teacher...	The Teacher...

Source: Personalize Learning, LLC.

Figure 1.3 PDI Descriptor Cards for the PDI Empty Cells Activity

provides instruction to an individual learner.	accommodates learning needs for the individual learner.	monitors learning based on Carnegie unit (seat time) and grade level.
supports groups of learners who are reliant on them for their learning.	Assessment **OF** and **FOR** Learning	adjusts learning needs for groups of learners.
actively participates in the design of their learning.	connects learning with interests, talents, passions, and aspirations.	is responsible for a variety of instruction for different groups of learners.
is responsible for modifying instruction based on the needs of the individual learner.	demonstrates mastery of content in a competency-based system.	Assessment **AS** and **FOR** Learning with minimal **OF** learning
identifies goals for their learning plan and benchmarks as they progress along their learning path with guidance from teacher.	owns and is responsible for their learning that includes their voice and choice on how and what they learn.	acquires the skills to select and use the appropriate technology and resources to support and enhance their learning.
designs instruction based on the learning needs of different groups of learners.	builds a network of peers, experts, and teachers to guide and support their learning.	uses data and assessments to modify instruction for groups of learners and provides feedback to individual learners to advance learning.
monitors learning based on Carnegie unit (seat time) and grade level.	understands the individual learner is dependent on them to support their learning.	identifies the same objectives for different groups of learners as they do for the whole class.

customizes instruction based on the learning needs of the individual learner.	selects technology and resources to support the learning needs of the individual learner.	selects technology and resources to support the learning needs of different groups of learners.
uses data and assessments to measure progress of what the individual learner learned and did not learn to decide next steps in their learning.	identifies the same objectives for all learners with specific objectives for individuals who receive one-on-one support.	becomes a self-directed, expert learner who monitors progress and reflects on learning based on mastery of content and skills.
Assessment **OF** Learning	drives their learning.	provides instruction to groups of learners.

Source: Personalize Learning, LLC.

Conversation Starters

- Compare your chart with the actual PDI chart.
  - Why did you select the descriptors that you did?
  - Why do you believe they fit where they are in the actual PDI chart?

- Review the PDI chart and discuss what stands out to you as the significant differences between personalization, differentiation, and individualization? Where do you see individualization but thought it was personalization?
- What is the learner experiencing in each column?
- How is teaching practice different in each column?
- How can you give voice and choice to your learners?
- In 25 words or less, describe to each other what the differences are between personalization, differentiation, and individualization.

SHARED VISION

How do you develop a shared vision of personalized learning?

Just like the phrase, *It takes a village,* it takes the whole school community and key stakeholders to develop a shared vision and belief system to transform teaching and learning.

Building personalized learning environments is all about the people in the community. We asked Virgel Hammonds, former Superintendent of Regional School Unit Two (RSU 2) in Central Maine, to share how his district pulled all stakeholders together around the district's vision. He wrote a post for us describing how the learning community moved from a traditional model to one that is highly personalized for each child and based on mastery, rather than on seat time.

It Takes a Village to Personalize Learning, in Maine and in Oz

Virgel Hammonds, Chief Learning Officer, KnowledgeWorks, former Superintendent, RSU 2, Maine

"Toto, I've a feeling we're not in Kansas anymore."

In 2007, the Maine legislature passed LD 2323, An Act to Remove Barriers to the Reorganization of School Administrative Units. The law was established to "ensure learning opportunities, rigorous academic programs, uniformity in delivering programs, a greater uniformity in tax rates, more efficient and effective use of limited resources, preservation of school choice and maximum opportunity to deliver services in an efficient manner." With this passage, the State of Maine was able to save $66 million annually, but it also forced highly independent school districts into shotgun weddings and forced marriages. A tornado of anxiety tore through the state.

Regional School Unit Two (RSU 2) administrators saw it as an opportunity to think differently about how RSU 2 educators could collectively support the unique needs of its 2,400 children living within this new, extended family. RSU 2 educators asked its learning community these questions:

1. What is our ultimate commitment to each child?

2. What are we preparing our children for?

3. How may each community member be a part of the solution?

4. How will the support of our learning community accelerate the growth of our children and our five towns?

Over the course of a year, the RSU 2 towns evolved from five, independent communities to one learning community that was focused on putting children at the center of all learning decisions. The RSU 2 learning community embraced learner voice and choice through varied learning opportunities that occur year-round and can take place inside and outside of schools. We worked collaboratively to support highly personalized, **competency-based** learning opportunities via community projects that needed new solutions, internships with community and state partners, experiential learning engagements nurtured by educators and community members alike, and through learning opportunities driven by children themselves. RSU 2 parents and business leaders wanted their high school graduates to be able to analyze and think critically, write and speak effectively, and collaboratively solve complex problems today and in the future. Equally important, the learning community requested children also be given the opportunity to learn at different paces based on the individual learning needs of each child.

Educators in RSU 2, and throughout the world, work tirelessly to support the needs of each child. To establish a highly personalized learning ecosystem, we cannot continue to solely depend on the miraculous measures of our educators. RSU 2's engagement of the community at large allowed for the exponential growth of learning supports available to children, educators, and families through community alignment and commitment. Though the consolidation law forced RSU 2 communities to collaborate, it also allowed them to think differently about their schools, children, and commitment to regional prosperity.

Tin Woodsman: What have you learned, Dorothy?

http://www.personalizelearning.com/2015/12/it-takes-village-to-personalize.html

Dorothy: If I ever go looking for my heart's desire again, I won't look any further than my own back yard. Because if it isn't there, I never really lost it to begin with!

Much like Dorothy, RSU 2 only had to look into its own backyard to realize its vision of a child-centered learning ecosystem.

Virgel Hammonds is serving the competency-education, personalized learning world in his new role as chief learning officer for KnowledgeWorks. He collaborates with thought leaders throughout the country to make the vision of an equitable, personalized, rigorous, and viable learning model possible for each child.

Personalized learning affects everyone in the community by changing how teachers teach and learners learn. In Activity 1.2, you can involve your "village" to help guide the process of moving to learner-centered environments.

ACTIVITY 1.2
Shared Vision: Group Activity for All Stakeholders

Ask everyone to download Tables 1.1 and 1.2 from the Companion Website so everyone has a copy to write on. You may want to put the tables on flip charts and give everyone Post-it notes or create a Google doc or other collaborative format. *[FYI: The link and passcode to the Companion Website is in the Introduction.]*

1. Invite all participants to contribute their current situations and where they want to be with personalized learning in 1, 2, or 3 years (or come up with a consensus from the group members on the date for their vision).

2. Have participants review the column under Personalization in the PDI chart and reflect on where they are now in their schools, districts, and communities as related to personalized learning.

3. Ask participants to write in the second column what they believe personalized learning could be like in their schools, districts, and communities.

Table 1.1   Current and Future

	Current Situation	Where You Want to Be
School		
District		
Community		

Source: Personalize Learning, LLC.

Use answers from Activity 1.2 to describe your current vision and then create new statements about what you wrote for "Where You Want to Be" to "New Ideas for Your Vision" in Table 1.2. Be certain that your vision ideas related to personalized learning effectively represent your desired outcomes for the learners in your school or district.

Table 1.2 Shared Vision

Current Vision	New Ideas for Your Vision

Source: Personalize Learning, LLC.

 Conversation Starters

1. How do these new ideas support your vision of personalized learning?

2. Discuss as a group any common threads.

3. Share any new ideas that inspire you and provide the desired out comes for your learners.

4. When you design a new vision on personalized learning, please share with us on the Companion Website.

At this point we want to share a school, EPiC Elementary in Liberty Public Schools, Missouri, that is an innovative, personalized, project-based learning community infused with technology designed to inspire learners to be creative and think big! Learners use real tools and real materials to collaboratively construct real-world applications of their knowledge. We asked Michelle Schmitz and Susan Maynor to share their story of how they built the common language around their vision and developed a set of beliefs that became established with everyone in their school community.

EPiC Elementary, Liberty Public Schools, Missouri

*Dr. Michelle Schmitz, Building Principal, and
Susan Maynor, Blended Learning Coach*

Our success as a school is built upon the foundation of shared leadership, both within and outside the organization, and the authentic process that constructed the components of our building and learning environment. In the spring of 2013, Liberty Public Schools established a 20/20 Vision Innovations Team, comprising administrators, teachers, parents, patrons, and board members to transform education for students. This journey began with the question, "What would you do if you could create the ideal learning environment to prepare students for a world that continues to evolve?"

Ideas developed around a 1:1 learning model with mobile technology, flexible learning spaces, creativity, team-based teaching, personalized learning, and authentic learning in the community. Leaders crossed the country and visited highly successful, innovative schools, specifically looking at best practices within high free and reduced lunch learning environments. The team tapped into experts, read research, and investigated different school models, ultimately discovering effective environments that empowered students to learn along with the elements needed for those environments:

- Real tools
- Authentic audiences
- Projects with meaning
- Personalized learning

The team then developed the vision and mission for EPiC Elementary and worked closely with an architect to design a flexible learning environment. Through this process, we learned that the birth of a vision requires the support of all stakeholders and the passion to make a difference for our learners. Our vision and mission provide a lens by which we continue to grow as a school.

We believe when students are engaged, achievement follows. The foundation of our school and our learner-centered system continues to rotate around and evolve from ideas generated from our stakeholders, both internal and external. It is essential we continue to include these stakeholders in our conversations and work. We share our story freely across all leaders and partner groups within our state and across the nation.

http://www.personalizelearning.com/2015/02/discover-epic-re-imagine-education.html

Dr. Michelle Schmitz is a passionate elementary principal who is reimagining and rethinking education to meet the needs of today's learner. Dr. Schmitz was a teacher for 10 years and then an administrator for 10 years.

*Susan Maynor is the **blended learning** coach for EPiC Elementary, a visual story-teller, design enthusiast, and creativity devotee on a quest to rethink education for all learners. She has taught elementary through high school, been a curriculum consultant, and produced various media for small companies.*

SHARED BELIEFS

In order to build a personalized learning system that is sustainable, a foundation of **shared beliefs** about learners, teachers, and learning communities needs to be established by all the stakeholders in the community. Each community needs to know and understand what the community values in the education of their children.

Examples of Beliefs:
Each and Every Learner

- can learn,
- learns at a different pace,
- needs to understand how he or she learns best, and
- needs to be validated for the way she or he learns.

Examples of Beliefs: Teachers

- see every child as a learner,
- understand how learners learn,
- relate to and build relationships with learners, and
- apply the current research on learning and metacognition in their practices.

Speck, who asserted that shaping a learning community is the most pressing task of the building principal, defined a learning community with the following description:

"A school *learning community* is one that promotes and values learning as an ongoing, active collaborative process with dynamic dialogue by teachers, students, staff, principal, parents, and the school community to improve the quality of learning and life within the school. Developing schools where every aspect of the community nourishes learning and helping everyone who comes into contact with the school to contribute to that learning community are important concepts" (Speck & Stollenwerk, 1999, p. 8).

As defined earlier by Speck, members of a learning community are mutually responsible for building the community. Thus, building a school learning community becomes the collective pursuit of the principal, teachers, students, parents, and all other community members.

Examples of Beliefs: Learning Communities (LC)

- believe that everyone in the community is a learner;
- include all stakeholders in a community who are equal partners in the education of their children; and
- recognize, encourage, and support change, risk-taking, and innovation.

ACTIVITY 1.3
Shared Beliefs

After developing a shared vision with Activity 1.2 and reading the stories from RSU 2 and EPiC Elementary, we want you to consider this activity to establish a shared belief system around each and every learner, your teachers, and your learning community.

This is a pair/share or small group activity. This activity is best done face-to-face so participants can brainstorm quickly. Post-it notes work well, or you can set up a Google doc with the charts. Table 1.3 can be downloaded from the Companion Website so each person can write his or her ideas first in the chart.

1. Have three flip charts on easels or create a collaborative document in Google docs that has the following headings:
   a. Each and every learner . . .
   b. Teachers . . .
   c. Learning Community (LC) . . .

2. Working in pairs or small groups, the groups discuss and add their ideas about how to complete the sentence on a Post-it note or add to the Google doc. Each group shares its ideas and places them on the relevant headings.

3. Move back to a whole group to review the responses and decide which ones represent the groups' shared beliefs.

4. Record the shared beliefs you agreed on in Table 1.3.

Table 1.3   Shared Beliefs

Learners	
Teachers	
Learning Community (LC)	

Source: Personalize Learning, LLC.

Conversation Starters

1. As you go through this guide, review your shared beliefs that you wrote here.

2. Update as you modify your beliefs.

3. Reflect on the question adapted from EPiC Elementary: "What would you do if you could create the ideal learning environment to prepare learners for a world that continues to evolve?"

4. Share any questions that you can use for reflection with your community on our Companion Website.

As we mentioned in the beginning of this chapter, personalized learning is a culture shift. It is about transforming teaching and learning. Every school or district is unique with different demographics, issues, and concerns. It is important to provide opportunities for all stakeholders to have a voice in this transition to personalized learning. We shared only two stories about a school and a district that involved all stakeholders and are sharing more on our website, www.personalizelearning.com—maybe we can include your story. What we have learned in this process is that it is all about relationships. Our next chapter describes how teachers can use Universal Design for Learning (UDL) Principles to build a relationship with each learner that is based on how she or he learns best.

 Build the Common Language

Building a common language around personalized learning is key in changing culture. We designed the Common Language activity that is included at the end of each chapter and have included a Padlet on the Companion Website so that you can compile the common language, communicate understandings about personalized learning, and begin to change the culture in your classroom, school, and district.

 Review: What did you learn that was new to you about the differences between personalization, differentiation, and individualization?

Learn: What new understandings did you discover when developing your vision and shared beliefs around teaching, learning, and the learning community?

Apply: How will you use the common language in developing your vision and shared beliefs?

2

How Learners
Learn Best

How do I understand how learners learn best?

Universal Design for Learning® (UDL) is a set of principles for curriculum development that provides equity for all individuals so they have opportunities to learn. UDL provides a framework for creating instructional goals, methods, materials, and assessments that work for everyone—not a single, one-size-fits-all solution but rather flexible approaches that can be customized and adjusted for individual needs. The takeaways in this chapter will be an understanding of UDL as the lens to personalize learning and how to develop expert learners.

UDL PRINCIPLES AND GUIDELINES

The UDL Principles provide a lens for teachers to understand how learners learn best. With this understanding, teachers are better informed about how to universally design their instruction in order to reduce barriers to learning as well as optimize the levels of support and

Consider This!

The UDL Guidelines can assist anyone who plans lessons to reduce barriers, as well as optimize levels of challenge and support, to meet the needs of all learners from the start. The UDL Guidelines are organized according to the three main principles of UDL that address representation, expression, and engagement.

National Center on Universal Design for Learning (2014).

challenge to meet the needs and interests of all learners in the classroom. Teachers use the UDL lens to understand how their learners learn best. How the learner uses the UDL lens will be illustrated and described in Chapter 4.

The Center for Applied Special Technology (CAST) developed the UDL Principles and Guidelines based on how each learner is unique and has **variability** in his or her learning (see Table 2.1). **Neuroscience** supports UDL by considering how individuals bring a variety of skills, needs, and interests to learning.

Table 2.1 The UDL Principles and Guidelines

Provide Multiple Means of Engagement	Provide Multiple Means of Representation	Provide Multiple Means of Action and Expression
Provide options for self-regulation	Provide options for comprehension	Provide options for executive functions
Provide options for sustaining effort and persistence	Provide options for language, mathematical expressions, and symbols	Provide options for expression and communication
Provide options for recruiting interest	Provide options for perception	Provide options for physical action

Source: Adapted from CAST Universal Design for Learning Principles and Guidelines (Meyer, Rose, & Gordon, 2014).

ACCESS, ENGAGE, AND EXPRESS

We came up with a clear and practical way of applying the UDL Principles for teachers to understand their learners and, in turn, in designing instructional methods and materials to meet the needs of all learners from the start. You will notice that our terms are different than in Table 2.1 and in a different order. The sequence was changed by CAST in its latest publication listed below Table 2.1. We prefer to use the UDL Principles defined by Access, Engage, and Express in the following order:

Access for Multiple Means of Representation

Engage for Multiple Means of Engagement

Express for Multiple Means of Action and Expressions

This lens is for all learners. It helps teachers understand how learners access information, engage with content, and express what they know and understand. Learners can also use this lens to understand how they learn best (refer to Chapter 4).

> As you're reading this chapter, we encourage you to think about how you access information, engage with content, and express what you know and understand—teachers are learners too!

When learners use this lens, it helps validate them as learners and it prompts conversations about their learning between the teacher and learner (see Figure 2.1).

Figure 2.1 Access, Engage, and Express

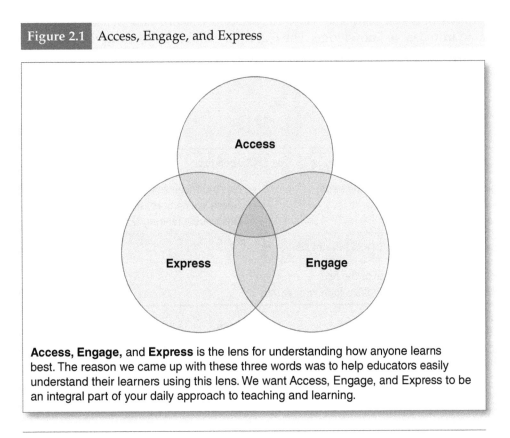

Access, Engage, and **Express** is the lens for understanding how anyone learns best. The reason we came up with these three words was to help educators easily understand their learners using this lens. We want Access, Engage, and Express to be an integral part of your daily approach to teaching and learning.

Source: Personalize Learning, LLC.

What does it mean to Access, Engage, and Express for learners? Table 2.2 helps translate the three terms as they relate to the learner.

Table 2.2 Access, Engage, and Express

Access	Engage	Express
by transforming information into usable knowledge through • digital media; • touch; • audio; and • visual media.	with content using • interactives; • video; • problem-solving; • designing; • self-assessment; and • reflection.	actions through • writing; • presenting; • storytelling; • multimedia; • building; and • making sense of learning.

Source: Personalize Learning, LLC.

Access

All learners are unique in how they access content and process information into usable knowledge. The example in Table 2.3 is from the teacher's perspective and reflection about one learner's strengths, challenges, and preferences and needs in accessing information.

Table 2.3 Access Example

Strengths	Challenges
• Good at explaining graphs and charts • Has a great vocabulary • Is an excellent reader	• Has a difficult time hearing • Doesn't remember what is being said • Has trouble reading text online
Preferences and Needs to Access Information	
• Prefers to read a hard copy of the text • Needs the instructions in written form with visuals	
Reflection	
Before meeting with the learner, I never realized how much trouble she had hearing me or remembering my instructions. I thought because she was an excellent reader, that she would not have trouble reading online. We worked together to figure out other ways to access instructions so she could read online.	

Source: Personalize Learning, LLC.

This example of access is about you understanding how a learner (not just a student) learns best. Everyone has strengths and challenges in how she or he accesses and processes information and turn it into usable knowledge.

Engage

Each learner engages with content and concepts using multiple strategies and tools that will keep her or his interest and encourage ownership of learning. We are all different when it comes to how we engage with content. This is the *affective* side of learning, helping learners understand their aspirations, talents, and interests.

Table 2.4 is an example of a teacher's perspective and reflection about one learner's strengths, challenges, preferences, and needs along with what personally engages that learner (aspirations, talents, and interests).

Table 2.4   Engage Example

Strengths		Challenges	
• Is great at teaching others • Is an excellent collaborator • Has outstanding leadership skills		• Gets distracted easily • Puts things off • Is shy • Has difficulty working in large groups	
Preferences and Needs to Engage With Content			
• Prefers to work in pairs • Needs to have a checklist to stay on task			
Interests	Talents		Aspirations
Is interested in creating videos with my cell phone	Knows how to use all types of technology and can explain how to use them to others		Wants to be a film producer or director
Reflection			
This learner is easy to work with, but I could never figure out why he could not stay on task. As soon as he started using a checklist and checking in with me, he was able to complete his work on time. After both of us realized that he wants to work in the film industry, he became animated when we did some research on the skills needed to be a director.			

Source: Personalize Learning, LLC.

Some learners learn best by doing hands-on activities to engage with content. Others may learn best by working alone and reflecting on their learning. Then others find they learn best when they collaborate with other learners.

Express

Now think how learners express what they know and understand through actions such as writing, acting, presenting, building, drawing, and sharing. Table 2.5 is an example from a teacher's perspective and reflection about one learner's strengths and challenges in how he expresses what he knows.

Table 2.5	Express Example

Strengths	Challenges
• Outstanding speaker • Great at multimedia and drawing • Strong problem-solver	• Has difficulty with follow through • Has problems organizing writing • Has trouble remembering details
Preferences and Needs to Express What They Know	
• Prefers to present ideas and projects orally • Needs a graphic organizer to support writing and multimedia projects	
Reflection	
I knew he was a great presenter, but after we talked, I also realized that he needed help with organizing his presentations. Most of his issues were because he tended to wait too long to put everything together and then panicked right before the presentation. We came up with him reviewing his draft with someone else who can give him constructive feedback.	

Source: Personalize Learning, LLC.

Some learners have difficulty expressing what they learned either because of self-confidence issues or even cultural concerns. They may be embarrassed about being in front of people or afraid to show off their work. They may even feel that they could have done a much better job because of wanting everything perfect.

Now that you have an understanding of the UDL lens, here is an activity that can give you a new insight to who you are as a learner.

ACTIVITY 2.1
How You Learn Best

Use Table 2.6 from the Companion Website to consider yourself as a learner and define your strengths and challenges in how you access and process information, how you engage with content, and how you express what you know and understand. Think about what your preferences and needs are in these three areas, knowing what your strengths and challenges are.

1. **Access:** When we asked teachers how they need or prefer to access information, some told us they needed pictures that illustrated the text or written step-by-step instructions. Some said they preferred to do their own research online. *What about you? How do you think you best access and process information?*

2. **Engage:** Teachers shared with us multiple ways they need or prefer to engage with content. Some teachers told us they loved collaborating through social media such as Twitter chats. A few told us they liked highlighting and taking notes as they do their research. Several teachers who said they needed quiet, but others needed music on. *What about you? How do you best engage with content?*

3. **Express:** This is where many teachers agreed that they are in this profession to share what they know with others. This came naturally to those who were comfortable with providing direct instruction. Others felt it was important to share what is happening in their classes by blogging, doing podcasts, and uploading videos to YouTube. *What about you? How do you best express what you know and understand?*

Table 2.6   How I Learn Best Template

	Strengths	Challenges	Preferences and Needs
Access	• •	• •	• •
Engage	• •	• •	• •
Express	• •	• •	• •
Words that describe me:			
Interests, talents, passions:			
Reflections:			

Source: Personalize Learning, LLC.

Conversation Starter

- What did you learn about yourself that you had not thought about before?
- How do you believe your new insight of yourself as a learner may affect your teaching practice?

DEVELOP THE EXPERT LEARNER

The UDL lens of Access, Engage, and Express is used so that teachers can understand how learners learn. With this knowledge, the teacher then can work with the learner in setting goals and acquiring the skills necessary to become an independent and self-directed learner—an **expert learner**. (Learn more about this process to develop expert learners in Chapter 4.)

> *"It is an important distinction for educators to know that they are not creating experts. They are creating learners who are capable of being self-directed and self-reflective."*
>
> Steve Nordmark

CAST reintroduced the **UDL Guidelines** (2014) in its publication *Universal Design for Learning: Theory and Practice* (Meyer, Rose, & Gordon, 2014). The Guidelines were redesigned to illustrate how an expert learner can be developed (Table 2.7). We added the headings in the top row to describe the progression as they relate to the UDL Guidelines. We included Access, Engage, and Express in the first column as they relate to the UDL Principles.

Table 2.7   Progression to Develop Expert Learners

	Accessibility for Variability in Learning	Guided Practice With Skills and Strategies	Independent and Self-Directed Practice	Expert Learners
Access (through multiple means)	Provide options for perception	Provide options for language, mathematical expressions, and symbols	Provide options for comprehension	**Resourceful, knowledgeable learners**
Engage (through multiple means)	Provide options for recruiting interest	Provide options for sustaining effort and persistence	Provide options for self-regulation	**Purposeful, motivated learners**
Express (and action through multiple means)	Provide options for physical practice	Provide options for expression and communication	Provide options for executive functions	**Strategic goal-oriented learners**

Source: Adapted from CAST, Universal Design for Learning Guidelines, *Universal Design for Learning: Theory and Practice* (2014).

Table 2.7 illustrates how you can use the UDL lens of Access, Engage, and Express and the UDL Guidelines to develop expert learners. Notice the progression that takes place from left to right where you begin thinking about how you can provide accessibility for the variability that your learners have in their learning. In the next progression, you want learners to develop specific skills and learning strategies to support their learning through guided practice. With daily independent and self-directed practice over time, the learner becomes resourceful and knowledgeable, purposeful and motivated, strategic and goal-directed—an expert learner. This progression will be explained more fully in the next section.

Expert Learner: Theory to Practice

The first question that may come to mind is what are the qualities of an expert learner? Table 2.8 describes those qualities of an expert learner.

Table 2.8 Qualities of Expert Learners

Expert Learners Are

Resourceful and Knowledgeable Learners by	Purposeful, Motivated, and Engaged Learners by	Strategic and Goal-Directed Learners by
• Bringing considerable prior knowledge to new learning • Activating prior knowledge to identify, organize, prioritize, and assimilate new learning • Recognizing the tools and resources that will help them find, structure, and remember new information • Knowing how to transform new information into meaningful and usable knowledge	• Having a purpose in their learning • Being eager for new learning • The mastery of learning itself • Knowing how to set challenging goals that push their learning • Knowing how to sustain effort and persistence that reaching goals will require • Monitoring and regulating emotional reactions that would be distractions to their successful learning	• Understanding their own strengths, challenges, and how they learn best • Developing their own personal learning plans • Monitoring their own progress as they learn • Devising effective strategies to optimize learning • Organizing tools and resources to facilitate their learning • Adjusting their learning when they realize that a strategy or plan is not effective
ACCESS The "What" of Learning	ENGAGE The "Why" of Learning	EXPRESS The "How" of Learning

Source: Adapted from CAST descriptions of expert learner in *Universal Design for Learning: Theory and Practice* (2014) and Personalize Learning, LLC qualities of an expert learner (2015).

Expert learners understand how to navigate their learning environments, where to seek out resources, and who to connect with in their personal learning networks to collaborate and consult with in any learning situation. Expert learners know how to learn from their mistakes and build new understandings. In Chapter 4, we'll discuss the process and the tools learners can use to become expert learners: the Learner Profile, Personal Learning Backpack, and Personal Learning Plan.

ACTIVITY 2.2
Qualities of the Expert Learner

 Activity 2.2 works best with groups of teachers, but you can do this individually to identify the qualities of the expert learner.

1. Invite teachers to work together in pairs or small groups to review both charts on expert learners.

2. Have teachers identify the expert learner qualities that they would like to see in their learners.

3. Discuss how UDL can be the lens for personalizing learning.

4. Answer this question and share in small groups: "How will you use UDL and the expert learner qualities to build a relationship with your learners?"

The idea of expert learners may be difficult to visualize. We invited Bill McGrath, who advocates for the use of UDL in Montgomery County Public Schools in Maryland, to share what it means for teachers and learners.

Pause/Think/Reflect

"UDL is just how we need to do the business of teaching and learning."

Bill McGrath

Where Are All the Expert Learners?

By Bill McGrath, Instructional Specialist,
Montgomery County Public Schools, Maryland

I work on a district-level team called HIAT (High Incident Accessible Technology) where we advocate the use of Universal Design for Learning as a critical framework to respond to the great diversity in our county. It has been a consistent and deliberate patchwork of seeding and growing UDL implementation projects with teachers, schools, and curriculum offices, never been a top-down district initiative.

When you see the various levels of UDL implemented in the classroom, right away you can see the benefits to learners. Impressive changes happen with levels of student engagement. Student on-task behavior improves. Students with more persistent and complicated learning barriers can have greater and more routine access to rigorous academic content. Teachers seem happier and better able to respond to diversity. UDL can look like a magic bullet.

As you walk into a classroom designed more along the UDL Principles, almost every observer notes a change in control. Students are driving more of the decisions in how learning takes place. There are varied pathways to instructional goals. These new routes are intended to be more efficient and avoid barriers to success. Our best teachers try to anticipate learners' preferences and needs, watch the varied learning that is taking place, and measure success toward learning goals in innovative ways. They adjust their subsequent learning designs based on new insights on the interaction of their learners with the more flexible design of learning.

By itself, giving students greater control to drive on roads that we think will be more engaging and accessible is not UDL. Students need hints on which routes may work for them and instruction to understand the road signs. Students may need to watch how we drive and hear us talk about our own driving so that they can understand effective thinking and problem-solving on the road. Students need time to share their experiences on the road with their peers and teachers to get fresh perspectives on new routes that may work better. Setting a goal that students learn to drive their own learning through active planning, reflection, and feedback is essential.

After a decade of watching UDL go from theory to practice in hundreds of classrooms, I have very little confidence that this learning to drive takes place in what we may describe as "UDL classrooms." We can get trapped in excitement by watching all the new driving by students. I worry that we are settling for just getting students behind the wheel. We need to ask ourselves if students are being taught to navigate independently and efficiently. We can lose sight of the goal for UDL: that each and every student becomes an expert learner.

The UDL framework gives us guidelines and a vision to build expert learners:

- Learners who can navigate flexible learning opportunities with great skill
- Learners who do not just navigate but are active partners and innovators in the design of future learning

UDL is a critical element of how we can respond with confidence and clarity. This needs to be a big part of our work right now and into the coming decade if we want to see the true potential of Universal Design for Learning. UDL tells us how to do this so it can work for each and every learner.

Strategies to Develop Expert Learners

Teachers can

1. **Make their intentions clear.** Tell learners you expect them to be expert learners. Explain what that means. Talk to teachers, parents, and district leaders about what this will look like. Set a clear expectation. Tell them to hold the UDL implementation process accountable for getting there.

2. **Be more curious than diagnostic with learners.** Expect to be surprised at how your learners learn best. Remember that this can vary significantly across environments and tasks. Know that the job of UDL implementation is for the learners to figure out themselves and act on that new self-knowledge effectively.

3. **Teach the language of expert learners.** Your learners don't know the language of being an expert learner, so teach it explicitly. Recognize that this is a language that can be adjusted for each learner at every age. It should include speech, writing, symbols, and nonverbal means of communication.

4. **Model metacognition constantly.** Expect teachers to routinely make their thinking behind UDL design transparent. Give them sentence starters to help them, such as framing choices with phrases such as, "so for me as a learner, I would . . ."

5. **Use UDL to teach UDL.** Your design for helping learners become expert learners by modeling, active learning, reflection, and feedback is like all other learning designs. It includes each and every learner. No one is left out.

Bill McGrath works on a district level team school called High Incident Accessible Technology (HIAT) where team members advocate the use of Universal Design for Learning as a critical framework to respond to the great diversity in Montgomery County Public Schools in Maryland.

UDL is not only the lens teachers can use to understand learners; it is also the lens for learners to understand how they learn best and how they can become expert learners. In Chapter 3, we introduce the elements of learner agency for becoming that expert learner. Each element will have a continuum that will help you understand how to develop self-directed learners with agency as they move from teacher-centered to learner-centered to learner-driven environments.

http://www.personalizelearning.com/2015/07/where-are-all-expert-learners.html

Build the Common Language

Add the common language to the list and Padlet that you started in Chapter 1 on the Companion Website.

- How can Access, Engage, and Express be used by teacher and learner?
- How can the common language from this chapter be used with the vision and shared beliefs from Chapter 1?
- How will you begin to use this common language with your colleagues in daily conversation?

Review: How does the UDL lens of Access, Engage, and Express change your perspective of the learners in your class?

Learn: How can the UDL lens of Access, Engage, and Express help you understand your learners and in creating expert learners?

Apply: How can the information you gathered from understanding a learner's strengths, challenges, preferences, and needs help you with your instruction?

Consider This!

Tomorrow when you arrive in your classroom, envision every child as a learner and then use the UDL lens to discover the learner in every child. Once you are aware of how each learner accesses information, engages with content, and expresses what he or she understands, then you are taking the first step in establishing a school culture where learners are valued and created.

3

Develop Learner Agency

How can you help learners develop agency to become self-regulated, expert learners?

In personalized learning environments, learners understand their strengths and challenges and are able to deploy learning strategies to support their learning. On a daily basis, they are developing the skills to be self-directed, self-regulated learners who are able to monitor their progress and make connections with prior learning. These learners can choose and use the appropriate technologies for the task and are motivated by mastering their own learning. If learners continue to learn in these environments, the anticipated results will be expert learners with agency who are truly prepared for their future.

They can develop the capacity to engage strategically in their learning without waiting to be directed. They can take ownership of and responsibility for their learning. And, they can possess the skills to learn independently, without heavy dependence on external structures and direction.

> We have a sense of **agency** when we feel in control of things that happen around us and when we feel that we can influence events. This is an important sense for learners to develop. Learners must understand
>
> * when they need new learning and how to learn what they need;
> * when they need to unlearn what will no longer serve them; and
> * when they need to relearn what they need to be successful.

"Spoon feeding in the long run teaches us nothing but the shape of the spoon."

E. M. Forster

There is a significant and growing demand for learners to be able to do more than receive instruction, follow a learning path designed by educators, and complete problems and assignments presented to them by an adult. Learners need to develop the capacity to shape and manage their learning without overreliance on the direction and control of others. Too often adults treat children as though they are incapable of making decisions or having their own valid opinions. As children advance through the system, they develop a form of "learned helplessness" that keeps them from advocating for themselves. The process for learning and the role learners play must be different than most adults experienced.

Seven elements contribute to learner agency: voice, choice, engagement, motivation, ownership, purpose, and self-efficacy (Figure 3.1). We arrived at these elements to define the journey learners of all ages can go

Figure 3.1   The Seven Elements of Learner Agency

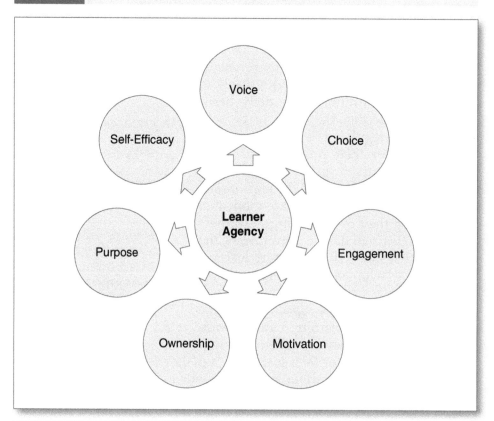

Source: Personalize Learning, LLC.

through to develop agency. Each element is a process defined along a continuum to guide teachers and learners as they move from teacher-centered to learner-centered to learner-driven environments. This terminology was taken from the Stages of Personalized Learning Environments (PLE) expanded in Chapter 8 and available on the inside back cover.

The takeaways in this chapter will be how each of the elements contributes to learner agency as learners take more responsibility for their learning. Each element includes its own continuum, which learners and teachers can refer to as learners move to agency.

VOICE

Learner voice gives learners a chance to share their opinions about something they believe in. There are so many aspects of "school" and "learning" where learners have not been given the opportunity to be active participants. Some learners, especially those who are concerned about extrinsic factors such as grades, may not feel comfortable expressing their own opinions.

Figure 3.2   Continuum of Voice

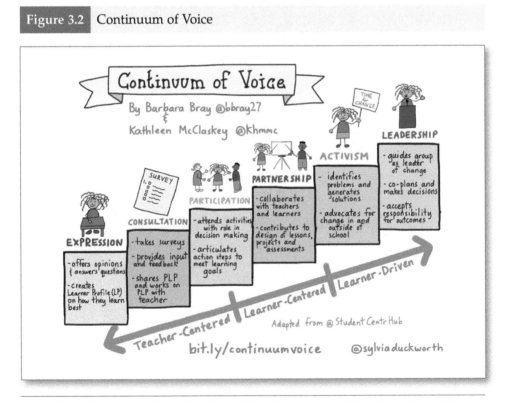

Source: Personalize Learning, LLC adapted from *Motivation, Engagement, & Student Voice* by Toshalis & Nakkula from Students at the Center @StudentCntrHub. Graphic designed by Sylvia Duckworth @sylviaduckworth. www.sylviaduckworth.com

Table 3.1   Continuum of Voice

Teacher-Centered ⟶		Learner-Centered ⟶		Learner-Driven ⟶	
Expression	Consultation	Participation	Partnership	Activism	Leadership
• Offers opinions and answers questions • Creates Learner Profile (LP) on how one learns best	• Takes surveys • Provides input and feedback • Shares LP and works on Personal Learning Plan (PLP) with teacher	• Attends activities with role in decision making • Articulates action steps to meet learning goals in PLP	• Collaborates with teachers and learners • Contributes to design of lessons, projects, and assessments	• Identifies problems and generates solutions • Advocates for change in and outside school	• Guides group as leader of change • Co-plans and makes decisions • Accepts responsibility for outcomes

Source: Personalize Learning, LLC, adapted from research from Toshalis and Nakkula, 2012.

Giving learners voice encourages them to participate in and eventually to own and drive their learning. Figure 3.2 and Table 3.1, the Continuum of Voice, illustrates a complete shift from the traditional approach where learners offer opinions to encouraging voice by guiding groups as leaders of change.

In their research paper, "Motivation, Engagement, and Student Voice," Eric Toshalis and Michael J. Nakkula (2012) from the Students at the Center explained in their spectrum on voice-oriented activities that learners can start articulating their perspectives as stakeholders in their learning to directing collective activities. They can move from offering opinions to being leaders of change. We adapted their continuum so it was more aligned with the Stages of PLE, which we'll discuss in more detail in Chapter 8.

Most learner voice activity in schools resides in expression, consultation, and participation. This is a process for teachers who were taught to be in control. This is the first element of agency and the toughest for teachers. This is where the research from Toshalis and Nakkula helped guide the process of moving from teacher-centered to learner-driven in a personalized learning environment.

> *Expression* is where the learners are used to being in a traditional teacher-directed setting. They raise their hands to answer questions and offer opinions when the teacher asks them. This is teacher-centered because the teacher guides the learners in creating their Learner Profiles (LP) to learn how they learn best.

Consultation is teacher-centered because the teacher is asking for more input and feedback as they guide the process. This is also when the teacher can sit down with the learners to get to know them and validate each of them as a learner. As they consult over the LP, the teacher can work with each learner by developing a Personal Learning Backpack (PLB) and begin the work of developing the Personal Learning Plan (PLP) to meet **learning goals**. We will be going over the LP, PLB, and PLP in more detail in Chapter 4.

www.personalizelearning
.com/2016/01/continuum-of-
voice-what-it-means-for.html

Participation is where the learners are developing more ownership as they participate in the learning process by identifying and articulating to their teacher how they plan to meet learning goals in the PLP. The learners have a more active role in decision making in the classroom that is becoming more learner-centered.

Partnership is where the learners are now more confident about how they learn and are more open to collaborating with others. The learners also want to contribute to what they learn in the design of lessons, projects, and assessments. The teacher and learners are becoming partners in learning.

Activism is when learners identify problems or challenges they might want to solve. When the learners realize they do not have a voice and that what they say matters, they can advocate for something they believe in. This is where the learners are starting to drive their learning in a learner-driven environment.

Leadership is when learners take voice to a different level and become leaders guiding the change process. The learners understand that having a voice can lead others that they can make actions happen and can take responsibility for the outcomes.

> **Pause/Think/Reflect**
>
> **Teachers:** *How can you add voice so you encourage more participation in your class?*

 Conversation Starters

- Why do you see Expression as the place to start building the relationship with learners?
- Why is it important for learners to have a voice in their learning?
- What can you do to encourage moving from Expression to Consultation and beyond?
- How do you see learners having a voice in a partnership role with teachers?

CHOICE

Providing choice can be confusing. Teachers believe if they create a menu of options that provides enough choices for their learners. If learners are choosing from a set of preplanned choices from a computer program or a list of options from the teacher, then the teacher is ultimately the one responsible for the learning, not the learners.

The goal is to move from being participants who choose from a menu of options to being self-directed learners who choose their purpose for learning. This takes time and a process for both the teacher and learners. Figure 3.3 and Table 3.2 show the roles learners can take as they practice demonstrating choice to guide their own learning.

Figure 3.3   Continuum of Choice

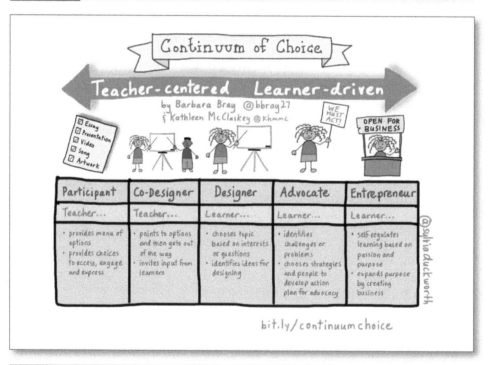

Source: **Personalize Learning, LLC with graphic design by Sylvia Duckworth**

Pause/Think/Reflect

"Call it personalizing learning or some other title, but in the end, we must make the very education that we are stewards of become about the kids that we teach again."

Pernille Ripp

Table 3.2   Continuum of Choice

Teacher-Centered → Learner-Centered ————→ Learner-Driven ——————————→				
Participant	Co-Designer	Designer	Advocate	Entrepreneur
Teacher	*Teacher*	*Learner*	*Learner*	*Learner*
• Provides menu of options • Provides choices to access, engage, and express	• Is a tour guide for options and then gets out of way • Invites input from learners	• Chooses topic based on interests or questions • Identifies ideas for designing activities, tasks, and roles for projects	• Identifies challenge or problem • Chooses strategies, resources, and people to develop action plan for advocacy	• Self-regulates learning based on passion and purpose • Expands purpose by inventing product or creating business

Source: Personalize Learning, LLC.

Participant: The teacher provides a menu of options for learners to learn content through images, videos, text-based resources, audio, hands-on activities, or interactions with peers. The learners showcase what he or she knows through different opportunities, from writing a paper to creating a performance.

Co-Designer: The teacher is a tour guide for learning possibilities and then gets out of the way so learners can go on their own journeys. The teacher collaborates with the learners to brainstorm ideas for lesson design, assessment strategies, and types of tools and resources to use with activities and demonstrate evidence of learning.

Designer: The learners choose topics and direction for what they plan to design based on personal interests and questions generated individually or with peers. The learners acquire the skills they need to choose the appropriate tools and resources for developing and creating their designs. The learners can guide the design of their learning to explore their interests, talents, and passions to discover their senses of purpose.

> **All instructional practices in this era of learning should revolve around learner voice and choice**
>
> Education works when people have opportunities to find and develop unaccessed or unknown voices and skills. Audre Lorde poignantly describes this "transformation of silence into language and action [as] an act of self-revelation." Opportunities for flexibility and choice assist learners in finding passion, voice, *and* revelation through their work. (Block, 2014)

www.personalizelearning
.com/2015/11/choice-is-more-
than-menu-of-options.html

Advocate: The learners choose a challenge or problem that they are passionate about. This is where the learners want to make a difference and persevere to choose what will be their purpose of learning. When the learners identify the challenge or problem, they then have an authentic voice with a clear purpose for the choices they will make to advocate for what they believe.

Entrepreneur: The learners self-direct and adjust learning based on what they want to do with their lives. They take their ideas and passions to create or join a business or cause. Even young learners may come up with an idea that improves a product or invent something that has never been done before. This is the driving force that becomes their purpose. The learners build a support system as their Personal Learning Network (PLN) that helps guide them on the journey to learn, build, design, create, develop, and promote an idea or product.

 Conversation Starters

- Why does providing a menu of options under the Participant level seem comfortable for most teachers?
- What can you do to encourage learners to move from Participant to Co-Designer?
- How do you see learners using choice as designers of their own learning?
- How can you see learners becoming advocates for their own learning?

ENGAGEMENT

Engagement has been found to be a robust predictor of learner performance and behavior in the classroom (Martin-Kniep, 2012). *Engagement* refers to the degree of attention, curiosity, interest, optimism, and passion that learners show when they are learning or being taught. When learners have a choice in what they are learning, especially if it is something they are passionate about or interested in, they jump in and sometimes get lost in the task or project. This is called *flow*. Figure 3.4 illustrates that when learners move from being in a compliant environment to one where they are in flow, you can see and hear the engagement.

Figure 3.4   Continuum of Engagement

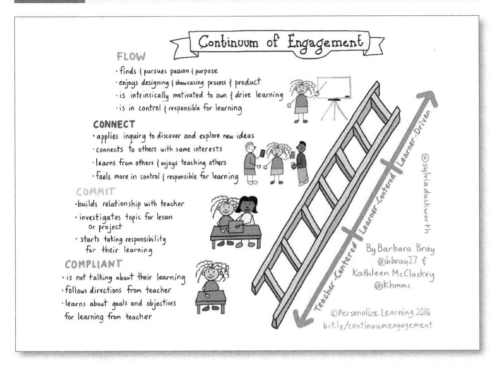

Source: Personalize Learning, LLC with graphic design by Sylvia Duckworth.

Mihaly Csikszentmihalyi is best known as the architect of the theory of flow. Flow is when learners are fully immersed in what they are doing because there is a balance and relationship between the challenge of the task and the skill of the learners that is illustrated in Figure 3.5. Flow cannot occur if the task is too easy or too difficult. Flow only occurs when the activity is a higher-than-average challenge and requires above-average skills. Both skill level and challenge level must be matched and high; if skill and challenge are low and matched, then apathy results. (Csikszentmihalyi, 1990).

When learners are engaged in the learning process, learning can sound and look "messy." How do we know learners are engaged? Engagement is a poorly defined concept in education. It is clear, however, that engagement is not simply about good classroom behavior or attendance, but a connection with learning. The learners who are quietly sitting at the back of the classroom not participating in discussions or completing their work are as disengaged as children who are talking with friends or others who did not show up at school. Fredricks, Blumenfeld, and Paris (2004) propose a framework that distinguishes emotional, cognitive, and behavioral engagement. *Emotional engagement* refers to the relationships between learners and their teachers, peers, and school.

The Continuum of Engagement in Table 3.3 provides the characteristics of learners as they move from being passive about learning to being in the flow.

Figure 3.5 Flow

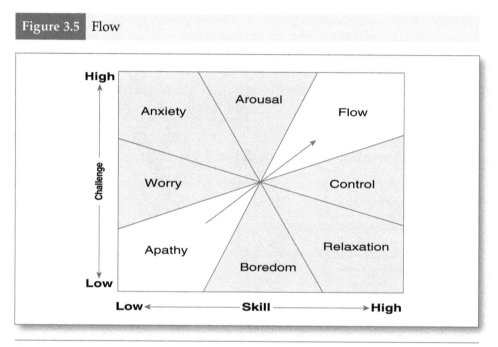

Source: Adapted from Csikszentmihalyi (1990).

Table 3.3 Continuum of Engagement

Teacher-Centered ⟶ Learner-Centered ⟶ Learner-Driven ⟶			
Compliant	**Commit**	**Connect**	**Flow**
• Is not talking about his or her learning • Follows directions from teacher • Learns about goals and objectives for learning from teacher	• Builds relationship with teacher • Investigates topic for lesson or project • Starts taking on responsibility for learning	• Applies inquiry to discover and explore new ideas • Connects to others with same interests • Learns from others and enjoys teaching others • Feels more in control and responsible for learning	• Finds and pursues passion and purpose • Enjoys designing and showcasing process and product • Is intrinsically motivated to own and drive learning • Is in control and responsible for learning

Source: Personalize Learning, LLC.

If you walked in a classroom, you might be able to see and hear engagement or the lack of it. In a *Compliant* level, the teacher is probably following the curriculum and doing what he or she knows or learned in his or her teacher education program. If a teacher is directing the learning, it might be to introduce a topic. Some activities are determined by the lesson. The teacher may have prepared the lesson, created or used existing materials for the walls, and set up the seating chart. Learners are rarely talking about their learning and are usually following directions from the teacher.

When learners are in the *Commit* level, they are committed in taking more responsibility for some of the tasks or skills they need to learn. The teacher may still be laying the groundwork for learning and determining prior knowledge at this level but the learners are more involved in what they learn. Learners may be in pairs, groups, or working individually, and the teacher could be walking around the room, sitting with one learner or meeting with a group. This is the level where the teacher is building the relationship with the learners.

When learners are in the *Connect* level, there is more dynamic interaction and sharing in the classroom. Learners are moving around the room, some are standing, and others may be sitting on the floor or in the hall. The teacher may have the same level of involvement as in the Commit level, but now the room is noisier in some areas while other learners are working quietly alone in another area. The learners are doing more of the talking than the teacher. This is where learners enjoy learning from each other and even teaching their peers. Learners are becoming more inquisitive by generating questions and investigating solutions to challenges, issues, and problems.

When learners are in the *flow*, this is called "messy learning." There is no way to capture what it might look like. There may be a few learners in the hall, some on phones contacting their mentors, two sitting together animated, a small group brainstorming in the corner, a few learners sitting with headphones on reading quietly, and some presenting their evidence to others for feedback. This is when learners are pursuing their interests, are curious, and are seeking what they are passionate about. You can hear it in their voices and actions. The learners know how to set goals and monitor their progress. The learners want to share what they learned and are motivated to take greater responsibility for their own learning.

www.personalizelearning
.com/2016/03/continuum-of-
engagement.html

Conversation Starters

Engagement: Review the article, "Interest Fuels Effortless Engagement,"
(Kaufman, 2014) available on the Companion Website

- Consider when you were engaged in learning or in the "flow." What do you remember about the experience?
- What words would you use to describe the activity?
- What does engagement look like in your classroom(s)?
- What are you doing now to encourage learners to be engaged in the learning process?
- How could you fashion learning activities so learners are challenged and matched to their level of skill?

MOTIVATION

Motivation has a great impact on the learning process. Some people learn more by outside influences, but others may achieve more by their personal aspirations. Figure 3.6 and Table 3.4 illustrate that in whatever the situation, everyone involved in any part of the learning process should know how motivation affects learning.

Motivation is what drives our behaviors. Extrinsic motivation occurs when we are motivated to perform a behavior or engage in an activity to earn a reward or avoid punishment. Intrinsic motivation involves engaging in behavior because it is personally rewarding; essentially, performing an activity for its own sake rather than for the desire for some external reward. Extrinsic and intrinsic motivation can also play significant roles in learning settings. Some experts argue that the traditional emphasis on external rewards such as grades, report cards, and gold stars undermines any existing intrinsic motivation that learners might have. Others suggest that these extrinsic motivators help learners feel more competent in the classroom, thus enhancing intrinsic motivation. (Cherry, 2016)

Fifty thousand years ago, the assumption about motivation was basic. Survival and biological needs drove all of our behaviors around gathering food and staying alive. As we formed more complex societies, we entered the industrial age where factories were designed with middle management. Workers were given specific tasks to do and received rewards such as salaries and benefits, or punishments such as cuts in salary or even termination of their employment.

Instrumental motivation is similar to the factory model that encouraged rewards and consequences. We are so used to this system that we are

Figure 3.6 Continuum of Motivation

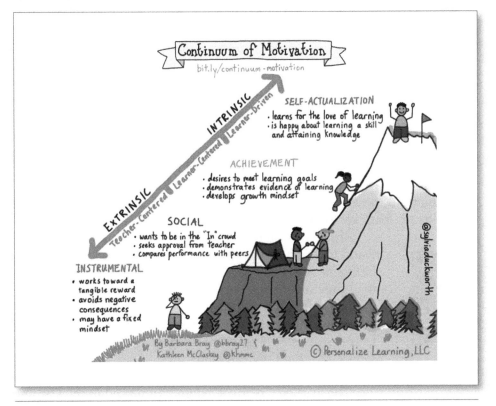

Source: Personalize Learning, LLC with graphic designed by Sylvia Duckworth.

Table 3.4 Continuum of Motivation

Extrinsic			Intrinsic
Teacher-Centered ⟶	Learner-Centered ⟶	Learner-Driven ⟶	
Instrumental	Social	Achievement	Self-Actualization
• Works toward a tangible reward • Avoids negative consequences • May have a fixed mindset	• Wants to be in the in-crowd to gain social acceptance • Seeks approval and to please teacher and/or parent • Measures and compares performance with peers	• Desires to succeed and to meet learning goals • Perseveres and demonstrates mastery with evidence of learning • Develops growth mindset	• Is involved and invested in learning for the love of learning • Derives satisfaction directly from understanding, learning a skill, attaining knowledge, creating something, or pursuing their purpose

Source: Personalize Learning, LLC.

comfortable with it and find it difficult to change. Students, especially high school students, may ask questions such as "What is my grade?" or "Is this going to be on the test?" Some students know how to "do" school to just get through. Others just want to follow the rules, and others are not motivated at all because they lost interest, are not successful, are bored with school, or feel no connections to the teacher, school, or learning.

When learners experience *Social* motivation, they want to be accepted as part of a group. Learners seek approval from peers and may want to please the teacher. The learners are motivated by looking good and measure how they perform with others, especially their peers. Friends may mean more to the learners than how they do in school. Learners are still motivated to learn by extrinsic factors.

www.personalizelearning
.com/2016/03/continuum-of-
motivation-moving-from.html

Achievement means the learners demonstrate that they want to learn and have a desire to succeed in school. Learners also want to work well and be successful more than they want to be part of the in-crowd. Learners choose the evidence that demonstrates mastery of learning and how they meet their learning goals. This is where the learners develop a growth **mindset** of believing in themselves and that they can learn.

Self-Actualization is about learners being invested in learning. The learners are involved and immersed in the learning process because of their love of learning. The learners could be learning a new skill, attaining new knowledge, or creating something that they never thought they could build. In Self-Actualization, it is more than just believing in themselves. The learners know they can learn anything they want if they put their hearts, minds, and souls in it.

 Conversation Starters

- How can you encourage learners to be active and interested in the learning process?
- How can you inspire learners to be more motivated to learn if they are only taking the class because they "have to?"
- What do you do with apathetic learners?
- How can you encourage learners to be invested in their learning?

OWNERSHIP

Chris Watkins, an independent consultant and leading authority on meta-learning in the United Kingdom and former reader at the Institute of

Education, London Centre for Leadership in Learning, has been a researcher on learning for the last two decades. In his research article, "Learners in the Driving Seat" (2009), he developed a metaphor to better understand the concept of "driving" our learning. When driving we have an idea for a destination—perhaps a bit of a map of the territory; we have hands on the wheel, steering—making decisions as the journey unfolds; and all this is crucially related to the core process of noticing how it's going and how that relates to where we want to be. Watkins makes these four points of what happens when learners drive their learning:

1. It leads to greater engagement and intrinsic motivation for them to want to learn.

2. Learners set a higher challenge for themselves.

3. Learners evaluate their own work.

4. Learners have better problem-solving skills.

The Continuum of Ownership (Figure 3.7 and Table 3.5) illustrates how learners move from compliancy to autonomy as they drive and own their learning.

Figure 3.7	Continuum of Ownership

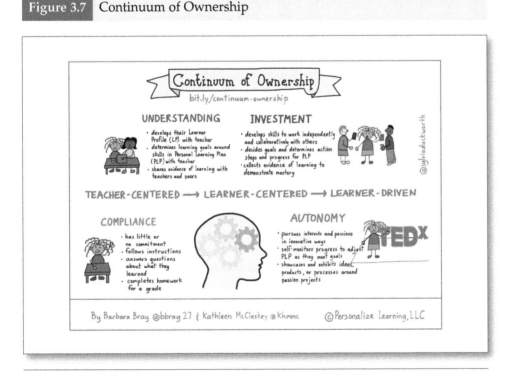

Source: Personalize Learning, LLC with graphic design by Sylvia Duckworth.

Table 3.5 Continuum of Ownership

Teacher-Centered → Learner-Centered ——→ Learner-Driven ——————————————→			
Compliance	Understanding	Investment	Autonomy
• Has little or no commitment • Follows instructions • Answers questions about how she or he learns • Completes homework for a grade	• Develops a Learner Profile (LP) with teacher • Determines learning goals around skills in Personal Learning Plan (PLP) with teacher • Shares evidence of learning with teacher and peers	• Develops skills to work independently and collaboratively with others • Decides goals and determines action steps and progress for PLP • Collects evidence of learning to demonstrate mastery	• Pursues interests and passions in innovative ways • Self-monitors progress to adjust LP as goals are met • showcases and exhibits ideas, products, or processes around passion projects

Source: Personalize Learning, LLC.

Barbara McCombs, PhD, from the University of Denver, states in her research *Developing Responsible and Autonomous Learners: A Key to Motivating Students* (2012) that motivation is related to whether learners have opportunities to be autonomous and to make important academic choices. Having choices allows children to feel that they have control or ownership over their own learning. This, in turn, helps them develop a sense of responsibility and self-motivation.

Compliance means that the learners do not own the learning, or may not believe they are the ones that have to do the work to learn. This is what most of us as learners experienced because "school" was designed for "students" to follow instructions. Since the late 1800s, school has been designed so that the teacher is responsible and accountable for learning. When you walk in a class where the teacher owns and drives the learning, the teacher usually tends to be the hardest-working person in the classroom. You will see walls covered with materials the teacher purchased or created. The teacher is doing most of the talking, and learners contribute to the class by doing what is asked of them.

In the *Understanding* phase, the learners share how they learn best with the teacher. In the next chapter, we'll introduce a new tool, the Learning Profile (LP), which will help learners think about and articulate how they learn best. Learners are given a voice by being able to share how they learn and their interests, talents, and aspirations. These conversations with the teacher help validate them as learners, which begins to shift responsibility for learning from the teacher to the learners. In this phase, the learners also consult with the teacher to determine their learning goals, for which we've provided the Personal Learning Plan (PLP). Learners share evidence of their learning with the teacher and peers.

Investment is when learners build confidence in developing the skills they need to work independently and with others. The learners see the value of goal setting and refer to their PLPs with guidance from the teacher to design their action steps. The learners are now more invested in learning and know how to identify and choose the best evidence that demonstrates mastery. Walking into a room where learners are invested in learning looks different. Learners are focused on completing tasks, talking about their learning, and excited about sharing the process and evidence of what they are learning.

Autonomy is when learners have the confidence and skills to work independently and with others. In using innovative and creative strategies, the learners extend their goals now to pursue interests, aspirations, and passions. Learners self-monitor progress as they adjust their PLPs while achieving goals. The learners identify and create passion projects that showcase and exhibit the process and products to peers, family, and possibly a global audience.

When learners feel a sense of ownership, they want to engage in academic tasks and persist in learning. If teachers and learners are learners first, then responsibility comes with being a learner. Learners of all ages become responsible for their learning when they own and drive their learning so they can be more independent and eventually self-directed learners.

www.personalizelearning
.com/2016/04/continuum-of-
ownership-developing.html

 Conversation Starters

Consider the following quote, and reflect on what it means to drive your learning: "As for the journey of life; at some point you will realize that YOU are the driver and you will drive!" by Steve Maraboli, "Life, the Truth, and Being Free" (n.d.).

- How can you encourage learners to be more responsible for their learning?
- How does providing choice encourage learners to have more ownership of their learning?
- Why is it important for learners to own their learning?

PURPOSE

The purpose of learning is about learners being prepared for their future and reaching their fullest potential as lifelong learners. This means that learners have a voice with the confidence to express their ideas and opinions so they are heard and taken into account. The Continuum of Purpose (Figure 3.8 and Table 3.6) is about learners establishing a clear purpose for learning and moving from conforming in a traditional system to making a difference.

| Figure. 3.8 | Continuum of Purpose |

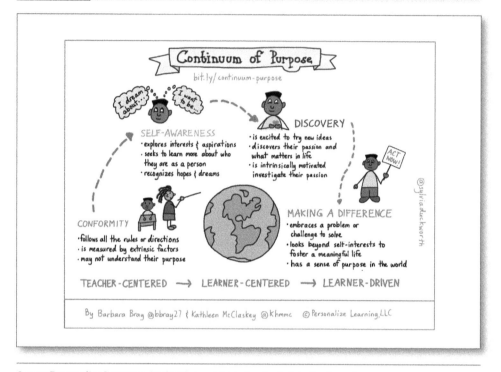

Source: Personalize Learning, LLC with graphic design by Sylvia Duckworth.

Establishing a clear purpose for learning encourages a desire to increase a deeper understanding of that purpose. In stating a purpose, learners can make their expectations for learning clear. Purpose goes beyond what we listed under Motivation because the learners are identifying challenges or problems based on some things they are passionate about. The whole sense of purpose is bigger than self. When you have a purpose, it has a broader reach, is self-fulfilling, and gives you a meaningful life.

"Your life has purpose. Your story is important. Your dreams count. Your voice matters. You were born to make an impact."

Australian Aboriginal Proverb

Conformity is when learners match their attitudes, beliefs, and behaviors to the other learners in the class. The learners tend to follow orders and are more concerned with what their peers believe. Learners feel peer pressure from the majority of the group. This can be called *groupthink*. The only purpose learners have is to conform to the group's purpose or other extrinsic factors such as grades.

Table 3.6 Continuum of Purpose

Teacher-Centered → Learner-Centered ————————————→ Learner-Driven ————————→			
Conformity	Self-Awareness	Discovery	Making a Difference
• Follows all the rules or directions • Is measured by extrinsic factors • May not understand his or her purpose	• Explores interests and aspirations • Seeks to learn more about who she or he is as a person • Recognizes hopes and dreams	• Is excited to try new ideas • Discovers her or his passion and what matters in life • Is intrinsically motivated to investigate that passion	• Embraces a problem or challenge to solve • Looks beyond self-interests to foster a meaningful life • Has a sense of purpose in the world

Source: Personalize Learning, LLC.

Self-Awareness is the capacity for introspection and the learners' abilities to recognize that they are separate from others. Learners seek to understand more about who they are by having a clear perception of their personalities, strengths, challenges, interests, talents, and aspirations. Learners also understand how other people perceive them and create opportunities to change behaviors and beliefs. The learners are just starting to recognize their hopes and dreams as the first step in determining what they may want for their lives.

In the *Discovery* phase, learners search for what matters in life for them. The learners are open to trying new things and taking risks so they can pursue and discover their passions. When learners realize that they can take control of learning around these passions, then they are intrinsically motivated to investigate everything about those passions.

www.personalizelearning.com/2016/06/continuum-of-purpose-fostering.html

When the learners find problems or challenges to solve, they are *Making a Difference*. This is where empathy comes into play. Learners look beyond their own self-interests to foster meaningful lives. They want to learn more because it is something they are interested in and passionate about. Learners want to make a difference by finding solutions to problems and tackling them. This gives them a sense of purpose in the world. When the learners have clearly stated and understood purposes, then they have the foundation for the process in building concepts, skills, and information.

> *"Efforts and courage are not enough without purpose and direction."*
>
> —John F. Kennedy

Conversation Starters

- How can you guide learners to develop their purposes to give them meaning in life?
- How could you connect academic efforts with real-world authentic activities?
- How can you create a learning environment so learners invest time and energy not in what is, but in what can be?

SELF-EFFICACY

The Continuum of **Self-Efficacy** (Figure 3.9 and Table 3.7) is when learners move from being cautious to building self-confidence so they can persevere to achieve any goal.

| Figure 3.9 | Continuum of Self-Efficacy |

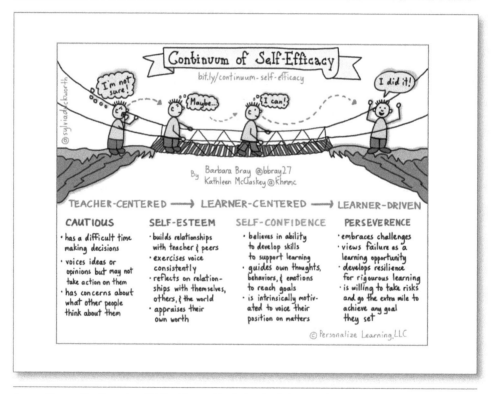

Source: Personalize Learning, LLC with graphic design by Sylvia Duckworth.

Self-efficacy holds significant implications both for learners and educators in the journey to nurture high levels of skill and knowledge. The most difficult and challenging learner to teach is the learner who believes he or she cannot succeed.

Table 3.7	Continuum of Self-Efficacy

Teacher-Centered → Learner-Centered → Learner-Driven →			
Cautious	**Self-Esteem**	**Self-Confidence**	**Perseverance**
• Has a difficult time making decisions • Voices ideas or opinions but may not act on them • Has concerns about what other people think about him or her	• Builds relationship with teacher and peers • Exercises voice consistently • Reflects on relationships with themselves, others, and the world • Appraises her or his own worth	• Believes in ability to develop skills to support learning • Guides own thoughts, behaviors, and emotions to reach goals • Is intrinsically motivated to voice a position on matters	• Embraces challenges • Views failure as a learning opportunity • Develops resilience for rigorous learning • Is willing to take risks and go the extra mile to achieve any goal set

Source: Personalize Learning, LLC.

For learners, developing challenging and complex skills and concepts are tasks to be avoided. If success does not come on the first attempt, these learners easily conclude that learning is not possible and then abandon their efforts (Bandura, 1986; Bandura, 1991). Often, learners with a low sense of self-efficacy try to hide and go unnoticed in classes or even misbehave and act out to avoid the embarrassment and pain of being exposed as not being able to learn what is expected of them.

Learners with a strong sense of self-efficacy approach complex and challenging learning tasks with a sense of confidence. If learners use good strategies, practice smart persistence, and use the full range of resources available to them, they can and will succeed (Wigfield & Wagner, 2005). The learners welcome challenges that stretch their capacity and build skills. When success is not immediate, the learners examine their strategies to see if there are more effective approaches to employ. The learners see missteps and setbacks as lessons from which to learn rather than as failures and signals to abandon the struggle.

Cautious is when learners have a difficult time making decisions and trouble believing in themselves. The teacher guides the decisions learners make as they voice ideas or opinions about something. Learners may have trouble taking action on any of the ideas they come up with. They may have concerns about what others think about them and are cautious about making any choices or stepping out of comfort zone.

Self-Esteem is when children start believing in themselves and becoming comfortable with who they are as learners. The learners are also reflecting on relationships with teachers, peers, family, and others in the world.

They feel better each time they share their voice and receive positive feedback. When they acquire the skills to make good choices to support learning, their self-esteem improves.

Self-Confidence is when learners believe in their ability, now that they have the skills to make good choices to support learning. Learners accept responsibility for all the choices they make and are intrinsically motivated to voice any concerns or positions on how they learn and other matters.

www.personalizelearning.
com/2016/05/continuum-of-
self-efficacy-path-to.html

Learners are confident in guiding their own thoughts, behaviors, and emotions in meeting learning goals.

Perseverance is when learners persist to solve problems or embrace challenges and develop resilience for rigorous learning. Some call it *tenacity* or *grit*, and the learners may even demonstrate stubbornness with a purpose. Failure is viewed as a learning opportunity. They are willing to take risks and are excited about going the extra miles to achieve any goal.

Conversation Starters

- How can you guide learners to build self-confidence about their learning?
- What can you do to help learners avoid being distracted while they learn?
- How can you encourage learners to take risks and demonstrate understanding beyond what is expected for a lesson?

We collaborated on a blog series on learner agency with the Institute for Personalized Learning. One of the blogs from Dr. James Rickabaugh helped explain why self-efficacy is the "secret sauce for learner agency."

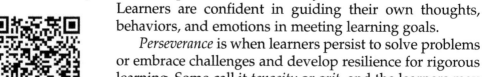

Self- Efficacy: Ten Strategies to Move to Personalized Learning

*Dr. James Rickabaugh, Director of the Institute for
Personalized Learning in Wisconsin*

Dr. Rickabaugh explained that many factors and experiences can undermine the strength of self-efficacy learners possess. The good news is that there is much we can do to reinforce and build self-efficacy. Here are ten strategies to get started:

1. Focus on learning as the goal by allowing flexibility in the pace at which learners are expected to learn. A "lockstep" approach to instruction can send the message to some learners that they are not capable when all they really need is more time.

2. Support learners to set short-term, attainable goals for their progress. When they have developed the confidence and capacity, guide them to focus and persist for longer periods on more challenging goals.

3. Coach learners to select and employ specific strategies as they engage in learning tasks. Have them reflect on and adjust their strategies based on progress and experience.

4. Compare learners' progress with their goals and current level of performance rather than with other learners.

5. Make feedback immediate and informative. Include guidance regarding next steps in the learning process. When we point out errors without accompanying feedback and guidance, we risk reinforcing what is wrong without providing a path to success.

6. Encourage learners to link their progress and performance to the strategies, efforts, and resources they employed. Guide them away from attributing success to some innate ability.

7. Delay the assignment of grades as long as practical in the learning cycle. When we assign grades to early learning attempts, we disadvantage learners who come without rich background knowledge and risk sending the message that they are not good learners.

8. Provide learners with peer learning models who will help them bolster and broaden their learning skills and strategies.

9. Where practical, give learners choices about their learning. This could include strategies to employ, timelines for completion, activities to demonstrate mastery, their learning team, or other dimensions of the work.

10. Be explicit in your belief about learners' potential and capacity to succeed. The four most powerful words we can say may be, "I believe in you." When learners feel our confidence and support, it is much easier for them to take learning risks and persist when they struggle.
(Rickabaugh, 2015)

Dr. James Rickabaugh is an author and forward thinker regarding personalized learning. His latest book, published by ASCD, is Tapping the Power of Personalized Learning: A Roadmap for School Leaders *(2016), which offers a blueprint that dramatically improves learner outcomes and prepares today's learners to meet life's challenges in college and beyond.*

www.personalizelearning
.com/2015/09/self-efficacy-
secret-sauce-to-learning.html

We provided the continuums of the seven elements of learner agency to help you visualize the process to guide learners to become self-directed, independent learners with agency. Chapter 4 walks you through how to discover the learner in every child using the Universal Design for Learning (UDL) lens of Access, Engage, and Express. This will help you understand your role in the relationship between you and the learners as they discover how to become expert learners with agency.

Build the Common Language

Add the common language to the list and Padlet that you started in Chapter 1 on the Companion Website.

- With the common language from continuums, where do you see your learners in the seven elements of learner agency?
- How do the continuums of the seven elements of learner agency connect with the previous chapter on the UDL lens and developing the expert learner?

Review: How could each of the elements of learner agency help guide the design of personalized learning environments?

Learn: How can the elements of learner agency help you understand your learners?

Apply: How would you use the continuums in deciding on activities in your lessons?

4

Discover the Learner in Every Child

How can learners understand how they learn best so teachers can discover the learner in every child?

When we enter the classroom each day, we need to see the learner in every child. In Chapter 2, we introduced you to the Universal Design for Learning (UDL) lens of Access, Engage, and Express so you can understand how learners learn. In this chapter, we introduce you to the process learners can use so they understand how they learn best. If applied, this process can help each learner develop the skills to become an expert learner with agency. It is also a way for each learner to become a proactive learner in her or his education.

This process can help learners determine how they best access information, engage with content, and express what they know to become expert learners: the Learner Profile (LP), Personal Learning Backpack (PLB), and Personal Learning Plan (PLP) as shown in Figure 4.1. Keep in mind throughout the chapter that when using this process, the conversations that you and your learners have about how they learn helps validate them as learners.

| Figure 4.1 | Process to Become an Expert Learner |

- **Learner Profile**
  - Strengths
  - Challenges
  - Preferences and Needs
  - Interests, Talents, Aspirations, and Passions

- **Personal Learning Backpack**
  - Tools, Apps, and Resources
  - Learning Skills and Strategies
  - Develop Learning Goals

- **Personal Learning Plan**
  - Learning Goals: Access, Engage, and Express
  - Personal Goal
  - College, Career, and Citizenship Goals

Source: Personalize Learning, LLC.

WHO I AM AS A LEARNER

Some children do not see themselves as learners. In fact, teachers may not see them as learners either. The LP helps learners articulate their strengths, challenges, preferences, and needs and helps learners tell their stories about how they learn. In addition, the LP opens the door for the teacher to have a conversation with each learner about how they learn best and what they are interested in or aspire to be. We've found that "Who I Am as a Learner" can be completed independently by most learners above the age of 9. With younger learners and learners with disabilities, we suggest involving parents or a counselor to help them think critically about themselves as learners. Listening to the learner, at whatever age, is an integral step in personalizing learning.

Every learner has a story so listen to his or her heart!

The LP can be reviewed and updated quarterly during the year to show how learners have progressed. We developed Table 4.1, "Who I Am as a Learner—Part 1," to help learners share their interests, talents, and aspirations. We recommend children do this section independently or with a parent/counselor—but without peer influence. This is truly where learners can finally tell stories their way. Teachers or parents can help guide younger learners or those who have difficulty reading or understanding the prompts.

> In this book, we've provided textual guides to complete this activity, where each learner is expected to *read* the questions and *write* responses. Teachers can provide UDL solutions for other ways to access the prompts to accommodate learners' interests, talents, passions, and aspirations. Consider a text-to-speech tool to read to the learner, audio notes for some learners to speak their responses, or another format that is accessible.

Table 4.1 Who I Am as Learner—Part 1

My Interests, Talents, Passions, and Aspirations
I am really interested in . . .
I like to do this in school . . .
For fun, I like to do . . .
If I could tell others one thing unique or special about me, that would be . . .
I am really good at . . .
I would like to learn how to be or do . . .
This really concerns me and I want to do something to make a difference about . . .
I have circled the words below that best represent me:
Creative, Curious, Funny, Social, Fearful, Apprehensive, Independent, Nerdy, Shy, Innovative, Entrepreneur, Risk-Taker, Intense, Follower, Leader, Out-of-Box Thinker, Bubbly, Quiet, Talented, Strong, Talkative, Athletic, Artistic, Calm, Perfectionist Geek, Intelligent, Introvert, Extrovert, Friendly, Listener, Determined, Stubborn, Focused, Thinker, Inquisitive, Skeptic, Outspoken, Self-Reliant, Nonconformist, Musical
Additional words to describe me:

Source: Personalize Learning, LLC.

ACTIVITY 4.1
Who I Am as a Learner—Part 1

Develop your own version of "Who I Am as a Learner—Part 1" for the learner. After Part 1 is completed, consult with the learner to review responses with you.

1. Here are some questions you can ask the learner: *Have you always been interested in . . . ? Were you surprised about the words you chose that best represent you? Did you find it easy or difficult to answer any of these sections? If so, why?*

2. Have the learner write a journal, record an audio file, audio clip, or video, a blog, or some other way to capture what they wrote in Part 1 to keep in their portfolios. Some other examples that you can use for reflection could include these: illustrate, draw, or paint; write a song or poem; make a photo collage, poster, or PowerPoint; or use a presentation app such as Explain Everything, Pictello, Story Creator, or Comics.

Conversation Starters

- How often would you ask learners to reflect on "Who I Am as a Learner—Part 1"?
- What technologies do you use for portfolios?
- How can you use the information they shared to engage your learners?

Who I Am as a Learner—Part 2

This section (Part 2) is in three parts using Access, Engage, and Express. The statements in the tables are for learners in Grade 4 and up. Once the learners respond in each section, we ask that they write or tell their stories around their strengths and challenges as they relate to Access, Engage, and Express. We then ask what their preferences and needs are in these three areas. When an individual has an opportunity to reflect and has conversations about how she or he learns best with the teacher, this helps validate the person as a learner.

> Some children may find "Who I Am as a Learner—Part 2" is difficult to do on their own. A teacher can guide the children as they fill it out or invite parents to provide feedback.

Access

Let's start with determining learners' strengths and challenges in how they might access information and then identify how they might prefer or need to access content based on their responses.

How I Access Information

Have learners use Table 4.2 to indicate the strengths and challenges in how they access information by checking all that applies to them.

Table 4.2 Access

Strengths	Challenges
I ask good questions.	I have trouble seeing.
I am motivated to learn.	I have trouble hearing.
I am very organized.	I often do not understand what I read.
I know how to use maps and charts.	I read slowly.
I understand what I read.	I have to reread information to understand.
I am a hands-on learner.	I have trouble summarizing what I read.
I learn by helping others.	I am not very organized.
I think differently than others do.	I cannot understand or read in English.
I am good at drawing and art projects.	I don't have confidence in my learning.
I explain math symbols and concepts.	I have trouble focusing.
I can visualize what I hear.	I cannot visualize the content.
I am willing to try new things.	I get distracted easily.
I am good with technology and mobile devices.	I don't understand what others are feeling or telling me.
I have good memorization skills.	I am uncomfortable asking for help.
I follow directions.	I don't understand oral directions.
I learn with multisensory learning.	I have trouble following written directions.
I connect to ideas I already know.	I am confused with technology.
I understand content with pictures.	I am not good at remembering things.
I am a good listener.	I have trouble finding what I need online.
I have an extensive vocabulary.	I have trouble understanding new vocabulary.
Add any other of your Strengths	**Add any other of your Challenges**

Based on your selections, tell a brief story about what you are good at and what is difficult or hard for you.

Describe how you prefer or need to access information. What helps you learn? What helps you read? What helps you remember?

List any tools, technology, or apps that you currently use or would like to use to access information and for learning.

Source: Personalize Learning, LLC.

Have the learners include the technology, tools, or apps they currently use or would like to learn how to use in the last section of this chart. If they aren't sure what tools are available to them, then this is where the conversations and relationships between the teacher and learners begin. Just imagine if a learner does not understand what they are reading. The teacher may recommend a text-to-speech tool and then the learner can reflect and share how it supports how to access and process information now that he or she can read the text. For ideas on tools or apps for Access, we have included a list on the Companion Website along with links on how to use some of the apps.

Engage

Next let's see how learners might want to engage with information and then have them identify how they might prefer or need to engage with content based on the responses. Again, have them write or record a brief narrative about their strengths and challenges.

How I Engage With Content

Have learners use Table 4.3 to indicate the strengths and challenges in how they engage with content by checking all that apply to them.

Teachers may need to help learners with ideas of technology, tools, and apps to engage with content. For example, if learners have poor organizational skills, the teacher can model a file management system. If learners already use a specific tool, they can list how that helps them engage with content and with learning. For ideas on tools or apps for Engage, we included a list on the Companion Website along with resources on how to use some of the apps.

Express

How do you know if learners understand what they are learning? Let's see how learners identify their strengths and challenges in expressing what they know and understand, and then have learners choose how they might prefer or need to express their ideas based on responses. Invite learners to write or record narratives that could tell stories about their strengths, challenges, preferences, and needs.

How I Express What I Know

Have the learners use Table 4.4 to indicate the strengths and challenges in how they express what they know by checking all that apply to them.

Just like you did with Access and Engage, you can consult with learners on their responses in Express. With each meeting with the learner, you build a relationship that gets stronger with every conversation. Again, you may need to give learners ideas of what technologies, tools, and apps they can use to express their learning. For example, let's say the learner has trouble organizing and putting thoughts on paper. The teacher can

(Text continues on page 67.)

Table 4.3   Engage

Strengths	Challenges
I am confident in learning.	I get discouraged and frustrated easily.
I learn well when I can stand or move.	I feel overwhelmed easily.
I like to research and look for answers.	I worry most of the time.
I put things together easily.	It is hard to get started on a new activity.
I like numbers and math.	I need help from teachers a lot.
I like learning new words.	I need directions repeated often.
I learn well while listening to music.	I need things to be perfect.
I get tasks done on time.	I don't like to study.
I am a good test taker.	I get bored fast.
I know what is important and what to do first.	I give up quickly.
I like talking and planning with others.	I don't expect to be successful.
I challenge myself to learn more.	I don't like doing difficult tasks.
I am an independent learner.	I am not good at managing my time.
I enjoy helping and teaching others.	I put off planning and finishing tasks.
I want to build things.	I can't say what I'm thinking very well.
I understand what someone else is feeling.	It is difficult for me to focus.
I am organized.	I have trouble doing independent work.
I manage my time well.	I have a few friends.
I have good problem-solving skills.	I get distracted and get off task easily.
I really focus on tasks when working.	I have low self-esteem.
I am engaged when doing what I like.	I don't always understand what others say to me.
I work well with others.	I have trouble working with others.
I know how to choose and use technology for any task.	I have trouble coping with many things at one time.
I like to lead others.	I joke around when working.
I am good at planning.	I have poor study skills.
I am not distracted by noise or disruptions when I work or play.	I have trouble sitting still and want to stand up or move.
I use an action plan to meet my learning goals.	I feel I don't always belong here.
Add any other of your Strengths	**Add any other of your Challenges**
Based on your selections above, tell a brief story about what you are good at and what is difficult or hard for you to engage in learning.	
Describe how you prefer or need to engage in learning. What helps keep you motivated to want to learn?	
List any tools, technologies, or apps that you currently use or would like to use to engage with content and in learning.	

Source: Personalize Learning, LLC.

Table 4.4   Express

Strengths	Challenges
I ask for help when I am working on a task.	It is hard for me to say what I am thinking.
I like using photos in my projects.	I feel anxious talking in front of the class.
I like to build models or projects.	I need help in starting a paper or story.
I like to present in front of the class.	I do not like to lead any group.
I like to write essays, stories, poetry, or songs.	I can't take notes and listen at the same time.
I am good at organizing and planning.	I have messy handwriting.
I can draw what I am thinking.	I feel uncomfortable asking for help.
I can manage information and resources.	I have a speech impairment.
I can explain things and retell a story well.	I have a writer's block.
I notice and reflect on what I am learning.	I have trouble putting thoughts to paper.
I participate in group and class discussions.	I do not feel comfortable starting a story.
I can create multimedia presentations.	I cannot speak or present in English.
I enjoy defending my position.	I cannot organize my ideas.
I like to show evidence of my learning.	I find note-taking difficult.
I am good at telling stories.	I cannot summarize what I read.
I use technology to communicate.	I do not reflect on what I learned.
I enjoy using social media, e.g., Facebook, Instagram, Twitter.	I know what I read, but cannot explain it well.
I am great at using interactive tools.	I cannot defend a position.
I am good at strategic problem-solving.	I am not good at drawing or illustrating.
I am a good presenter and speaker.	I do not feel good about setting goals.
I can keep track of my learning.	I have a difficult time using technology.
I can manage information and resources.	I do not write descriptively.
I feel confident about sharing my ideas.	I feel anxious when I take a test.
Add any other of your Strengths	**Add any other of your Challenges**

Based on your selections, tell your story about your about what you are good at and what is difficult or hard for you to express what you know and understand.

Describe how you prefer or need to express what you know and understand.

List any technology, tools, or apps that you currently use or would like to use express what you know and understand.

Source: Personalize Learning, LLC.

introduce visual graphic organizers to brainstorm and organize ideas and a speech-to-text tool or app for the learner to use to write her or his thoughts.

We will be sharing examples of technology, tools, and apps along with video tutorials that address Access, Engage, and Express to include in the PLB and in goal setting in the PLP later in this chapter and on the Companion Website.

ACTIVITY 4.2
Who I Am as a Learner—Part 2

 Personalize your own version of "Who I Am as a Learner—Part 2" and have the learner complete each section. After the learner completes all three sections, schedule a meeting to review the strengths, challenges, preferences, and needs in Access, Engage, and Express. Ask the learner these questions:

1. What stood out from your stories in each of the sections?

2. What was difficult or hard for you? What was easy?

3. How did you decide what you prefer or need for learning?

4. What questions do you have about what you found out about yourself?

 Conversation Starters

- Other teachers will be reading this book, so what would you like to share with them about this process as learners completed the "Who I Am as a Learner?" activity?
- How did the conversations build a better relationship with your learners?
- How do you see this process validating the learners and how they feel about themselves as a learner and learning?

LEARNER PROFILE (LP)

After the learner completes "Who I Am as a Learner," Parts 1 and 2, the next step is to create the **Learner Profile (LP)** using the LP template, which indicates the learner's key strengths, challenges, preferences, and needs along with their interests, talents, and aspirations. The learners take what they included in these sections of "Who I Am as a Learner" and place them into the LP. We suggest that the LP be reviewed at least quarterly because strengths and challenges will change. Maintaining a record of the LP is important so that the learner can monitor their progress. You may want to consider a folder and file system where you can maintain records and review the progress of the LP from year to year with each learner.

We created a LP for a learner who struggled as a reader since first grade and had an Individual Education Plan (IEP) created by the IEP team. The IEP focused on the child's weaknesses in reading, writing, and organizing. The IEP stated how the teacher could accommodate those challenges in the classroom instead of focusing on building skills to support his challenges and around his strengths to adapt his learning strategies in areas where he experienced difficulty. The template for Table 4.5 is available on the Companion Website.

Table 4.5   Example Learner Profile

Name:			Date:
	Strengths	**Challenges**	**Preferences and Needs**
Access	• I can visualize what I hear. • I connect to ideas I already know.	• I often do not understand what I read. • I have trouble focusing.	• I need to use a text-to-speech tool for reading. • I prefer to use video for understanding.
Engage	• I like to lead others. • I work well with others.	• I don't like doing difficult tasks.	• I need tasks to be broken down into smaller tasks. • I prefer to work with a partner.
Express	• I draw what I am thinking. • I like telling stories orally. • I am a good presenter and speaker.	• I have trouble putting thoughts to paper. • I find note-taking is difficult.	• I need to use a note-taking tool. • I prefer graphic organizers to help me organize ideas. • I prefer to present orally.

Words that describe me: Curious, Imaginative, Independent, Artistic, Friendly, Optimist

Interests, talents, and passions: I am interested in soccer, baseball, and history. I am talented in storytelling, interpersonal skills, drawing, connecting the dots, and mental math. I am passionate about fishing and having my own business one day that helps people.

Reflections: I am really happy I got to do this Learner Profile and share it with my teacher. I like that my teacher knows what I'm interested in and listened to me during our talk.

Source: Personalize Learning, LLC.

The LP in Table 4.5 was developed with input from that learner where he identified his strengths, interests and challenges and what he preferred or needed to learn as it related to Access, Engage, and Express. The outcome was a learner who not only articulated what he needed, but felt that he had a voice in how he learned best and what he needed to become more independent.

He never saw himself as a learner until he completed the LP. When the teacher consulted with this learner, it was the first time he was able to tell his story about how he learns and what he thinks he needs to learn. This experience changed the perspectives of both the teacher and the learner. The LP helps the teacher and the learner build a relationship based on trust. When you have learners share who they are as learners with the LP, you are telling them that you care about them.

> As you review each learner's LP, consider his or her social and emotional needs along with prior knowledge. Teachers also need to consider culturally responsive teaching that acknowledges, responds to, and celebrates a variety of cultures and offers full, equitable access to education for learners from all cultures. [Education Alliance at Brown University]

PERSONAL LEARNING BACKPACK (PLB)

Once a learner has indicated strengths and challenges along with preferences and needs to Access, Engage, and Express, then the teacher and learner begin to work on developing a **Personal Learning Backpack (PLB)**. The PLB will include the tools, apps, and resources that could be used to support learning, as well as the learning strategies and skills that help them become an independent expert learner.

If the learner has indicated in their LP that she or he would like to learn how to use a tool or app to support a strength or challenge the learner may have, then this could be included as a learning goal in her or his PLP found later in this chapter.

We took the LP of the learner we described previously and added the PLB in Table 4.6 to describe the tools, learning strategies, and skills this learner will need to support his own learning independently.

Table 4.6   Example of a Learner Profile and Personal Learning Backpack

Name:				Date:
Learner Profile				**Personal Learning Backpack**
	Strengths	**Challenges**	**Preferences and Needs**	**Tools, Apps, Resources; Learning Strategies/Skills**
Access	• I can visualize what I hear. • I connect to ideas I already know.	• I often do not understand what I read. • I have trouble focusing.	• I need to use a text-to-speech tool for reading. • I prefer to use video for understanding.	I would like to explore audio/text-to-speech for reading and comprehension as well as font options and access to my learning materials in digital format to use on my laptop/tablet, etc.
Engage	• I like to lead others. • I work well with others.	• I don't like doing difficult tasks.	• I need tasks to be broken down into smaller tasks. • I prefer to work with a partner.	I like working with a peer who knows how to help me break down tasks on projects. I like having a video that provides step-by-step instructions on developing new skills. I like a picture schedule or calendar with reminders that can help me to organize and stay on task.
Express	• I draw well. • I like telling stories orally. • I am a good presenter and speaker.	• I have trouble putting thoughts to paper. • I find note taking is difficult.	• I need to use a note taking tool. • I prefer graphic organizers to help me organize ideas. • I prefer to present orally.	I would like to use an audio recording app/technology to help me take notes and listen at the same time. I would like an app to help me brainstorm and organize ideas for writing. I would like to use multimedia where I can present information with audio, video, and/or drawings. I would like to be independent with finding mistakes and editing using word prediction or speech-to-text technology.
Words about me: Curious, Imaginative, Independent, Artistic, Friendly, Optimist				
Interests, talents, and passions: Interested in soccer, baseball, and history. I am talented in storytelling, interpersonal skills, drawing, connecting the dots, and mental math. I am passionate about fishing and having my own business one day that helps people.				

Source: Personalize Learning, LLC.

The learners can use the LP and PLB Template (Table 4.7) to describe the tools, learning strategies, and skills they will need to support their learning independently. This template is available for download on the Companion Website.

Table 4.7 Learner Profile and Personal Learning Backpack Template

Name:				Date:
Learner Profile				**Personal Learning Backpack**
	Strengths	Challenges	Preferences and Needs	Tools, Apps, Resources; Learning Strategies/Skills
Access				
Engage				
Express				
Words about me:				
Interests, talents, and passions:				

Source: Personalize Learning, LLC.

ACTIVITY 4.3
Learner Profile and Personal Learning Backpack

Now let's look at how your learner can create his or her LP and PLB. This is where the conversations begin. If you are unfamiliar with tools or apps, please refer to the Companion Website for ideas that could be included in the PLB.

1. Take the completed "Who I Am as a Learner" Parts 1 and 2 documents and have your learners:
   a. Indicate the strengths and challenges that they have in Access, Engage, and Express. If there are more than five, have the learners include the five that best describe their top strengths and challenges.
   b. List the words that best describe them in "Words about me."
   c. Describe their interests, talents, and aspirations.

2. Once that is completed, have a conversation with your learners:
   a. On the types of tools, apps, and resources that they currently use or would like to use to support their strengths or challenges; and
   b. On the skills that they would like to develop with the tools, apps, and resources so that they can be more independent in learning.

Conversation Starters

- What did you discover about your learners that you did not know before developing the PLB?
- What new apps, tools, and resources did you discover in the conversation with your learners?
- How did you both decide how to use the learner's strengths to support the learner's challenges?

PERSONAL LEARNING PLAN (PLP)

The purpose of the **Personal Learning Plan (PLP)** is to assist each learner in developing independent learning skills, personal goals, and college, career, and citizenship goals with a set of actionable steps to achieve those goals. The PLP has four areas of focus with the intent for the learner to develop agency with a direction for their future along with becoming an active citizen in the local and global community:

- Access, Engage, and Express Goals for Skill Development—derived from the LP and PLB
- Personal Goals—derived from their interests, talents, aspirations, and passions or something they want to learn how to do

- College and Career Goals—derived from discussions with advisors, counselors, and parents and personal goals they have experienced
- Citizenship Goals—derived from an interest or passion on how they can make a difference in the local or global community

The PLP is where the learners, in conjunction with the teacher or advisor, decide on their goals, what steps to take to achieve their goals, and how to measure progress. Goal setting is an important skill that can result in increased motivation and perseverance. Remember that having a realistic step-by-step action plan for the goal and a way to measure progress is key in having a learner achieve it. With each goal, the learners need to reflect on the goal and the process they took to achieve it. Consider placing the evidence of achievement in a learner portfolio along with reflections so the learners have a record of their achievements.

How can learners develop a PLP to develop skills to be future ready?

Access, Engage, and Express Goals for Skill Development

The first section of the PLP includes Access, Engage, and Express goals so that the learner can develop independent skills to support his or her own learning. The learner and the teacher/advisor collaborate on the plan to outline the *action steps* to reach the goal(s) and indicate evidence in achieving the goal(s) along with a date it was achieved. For each goal, they include any supports that will be needed to achieve the goal. We have included a set of apps or tools that can support them in each of the examples for Access, Engage, and Express.

> Action steps can direct the learners to take action and not be just a part of a "to do" list. Each action step needs to begin with a verb—for example, "Schedule time to learn Popplet with the technology coach" or "Learn how to create a folder and file system for my projects."

There can be more than one goal in each area, and in some cases, learners may not have a goal in one or more areas of Access, Engage, and Express. Once a goal is achieved, the learner reflects on achieving the goal(s) and indicates the date the goal was achieved. We also recommend that the learner post evidence of reaching the goal(s) in a **Learner Portfolio**. We have taken each goal area and created an example for each type of goal in Tables 4.8, 4.9, and 4.10.

Table 4.8   Example of PLP—Access Goal

My Personal Learning Plan Name:		Progress
Access Goal 1	I want to learn how to use text-to-speech technology and/or apps to support my reading and comprehension of learning materials and texts.	**Evidence of reaching my goal:** • Completing comprehension questions or an assignment (video/poster/paper) using technologies or tools independently from the backpack. • Demonstration of independent reading using the tools. **Date Achieved:**
Steps **Date added:**	Action steps that will help meet my goal: 1. Set a schedule to work with my technology coach or a peer tutor to learn the text-to-speech technology and/or apps. 2. Read textbook, handout, assigned novel, or online content using text-to-speech technology and/or apps. 3. Learn and apply comprehension strategies using highlighting and mind-mapping and supportive writing tools.	

Other supports I will need for my Access Goal: Accessible Educational Materials (AEM), digital books, and handouts to use with technologies and tools.

Set of apps/tools that could support my Access Goal: Speech-to-text tools, audiobooks, text-to-speech tools, word prediction tools, audio recordings, note-taking support tools, mind-mapping tools (e.g., Voice Dream Reader, Notability, Read&Write, ClaroPDF, LucidChart for Education, Inspiration app and software, Ginger, and Grammarly). These apps and technologies are available for iOS/Google Chrome, all platforms and devices. See Companion Website for other suggestions.

Reflection on achieving my Access Goal 1:

I had trouble understanding what I was reading. I discussed this issue with my teacher, who suggested trying a text-to-speech tool. After I learned how to use an app that read to me, it made it so much easier for me to understand what I was reading.

Source: Personalize Learning, LLC.

This particular learner has spent many years not accessing printed materials, textbooks, and assigned books because of his inability to decode words. He has regular instruction in reading by an **Orton-Gillingham–trained** reading teacher, but his fluency is not at grade level and his comprehension has been affected. A text-to-speech tool or app was selected by the teacher and learner to support his ability to independently access reading materials and text and to help him develop comprehension skills.

Table 4.9 Example of PLP—Engage Goal

My Personal Learning Plan Name:		Progress
Engage Goal 1	I want to learn how to break down activities and assignments into smaller tasks so I can start and finish an assignment on time.	**Evidence of reaching my goal:** • Complete an assignment on time for a project that I organized into smaller tasks. • Submit a copy of completed organization tool or graphic organizer. **Date Achieved:**
Steps **Date added:**	Action steps that will help meet my goal: 1. Use visual tools and technologies to map out my tasks and due dates (Action Plan). 2. Learn how to use a file and folder system to manage my resources, projects, and assignments. 3. Initiate and complete tasks, use checklists and data tracking tools.	

Other supports I will need for my Engage Goal: Quiet location to organize and map out my tasks; check in with teacher on any guidance I may need. Access to digital or tactile graphic organizers, visual templates.

Set of apps/tools that could support my Engage Goal: Folder and file management tools, time and task tools or apps: (e.g., Google Drive, Evernote, Dropbox, Toodledo, ToDo List, LucidChart for Education, Connected Mind, Inspiration) These apps/technologies are available for iOS/Google Chrome, all platforms and devices. See Companion Website for other suggestions.

Reflection on achieving my Engage Goal 1:

I always had problems organizing my assignments. Now that I know how to manage my files and use a checklist, I'm able to monitor my progress and keep better track of each task.

Source: Personalize Learning, LLC.

This learner realized he had a challenge organizing materials and information especially when given an assignment or project to do. The focus for this goal was to develop the skills he will need to use the tools or apps that will help him breakdown and map out his tasks for a project. Another skill he will need to learn is to monitor and track his own progress in meeting this goal.

Table 4.10   Example of PLP—Express Goal

My Personal Learning Plan Name:		Progress
Express Goal 1	I want to learn to use mind-mapping tools to organize and present my ideas and knowledge using multimedia and technologies/tools.	**Evidence of reaching my goal:** • Plan, organize, and present a multimedia presentation for a project
Steps **Date added:**	Action steps that will help meet my goal: 1. Learn to use mind-mapping/brainstorming tools and graphic organizers. 2. Learn to use multimedia presentation tools with audio, video, narration, etc.	**Date Achieved:**

Other supports I will need for my Express Goal: Options for presenting my knowledge other than written format. Access to technologies and tools to complete my presentation.

Set of apps/tools that could support my Express Goal: mind-mapping tools or apps, multimedia tools or apps, audio recording tools: (e.g., Popplet, Connected Mind, Inspiration, LucidChart for Education, Explain Everything, Book Creator, Pictello, iMovie) These apps/technologies are available for iOS/Google Chrome, all platforms and devices. See Companion Website for other suggestions.

Reflection on achieving my Express Goal 1:

I had difficulty pulling my presentations together so they made sense. Mind-mapping tools really helped me organize my ideas. I also found ways to add videos and audio files so it made my presentations more interesting and personal for my audience.

Source: Personalize Learning, LLC.

Learners can even consider expanding skills around a strength when deciding on a goal. This learner shared that one of his strengths is presenting to a group. He wanted to learn how to use tools or apps that would enhance his presentation skills and help him organize his presentation which also addresses one of his challenges.

Personal Goals

This is where the learner includes any personal goals he may have. These could be based on an interest, talent, aspiration, or passion, and these could also include something the learner would just like to learn. This goal could be conducted inside or outside of school. In the example in Table 4.11, the learner would like to learn more about the Revolutionary War, an interest that he has had for several years.

Table 4.11   Example of PLP—Personal Goal

My Personal Learning Plan Name:		Progress
Personal Goal 1	I would like to interview an historian about the Revolutionary War.	**Evidence of reaching my goal:**
Steps **Date added:**	Action steps that will help meet my goal: 1. Perform a search of Revolutionary War historians that may live in the state or New England region. 2. Locate the historian and coordinate a time to interview him/her. Request to do an audio recording. 3. Prepare questions for the interview and review with my teacher(s). 4. Conduct interview with the historian. 5. Follow up with a thank you letter and/or email.	• Conduct the interview and send a thank you note. • Reflect in my Learner Portfolio about this experience. • Present information from interview. **Date Achieved:**
Other supports I will need for my Personal Goal: Request help from my advisor or teacher how to begin locating a Revolutionary War historian. Role playing, interview questions, practice with my advisor or teacher on interview process for historian.		
Set of apps/tools that could support my Personal Goal: portfolio or learning journal tool or app: (e.g., SeeSaw app (learning journal); Google Docs, Evernote, Dropbox, LiveBinders, Google Drive, Pages) These apps/technologies are available for iOS/Google Chrome, all platforms and devices. See Companion Website for other suggestions.		
Reflection on achieving my Personal Goal 1: It was so great to actually interview someone who studied the Revolutionary War. I'm grateful that my teacher helped me create the questions for the interview and then found someone who was so excited about sharing what he knew about the Revolutionary War.		

Source: Personalize Learning, LLC.

College and Career Goals

College and career goals in the early years may be exploratory in nature for a number of years. Some learners will have a clear direction of what they want to do by high school, but others will want to have experiences based on their interests, talents, aspirations, or passions. In some areas in the United States, these are called **Extended Learning Opportunities** (ELOs), where the learner is paired with a mentor in a work or business environment so he or she gains insight and experiences in a field they may be interested in. Some high schools offer programs where the learner designs her or his own pathways to graduation. In these programs, she or he can participate as an apprentice or take online high school or college courses. Each of these experiences will prepare the learner to be future ready for college, career, and life (see Table 4.12).

Table 4.12   Example of PLP—College and Career Goal

My Personal Learning Plan Name:		Progress
College and Career Goal 1	I would like to have an ELO on what it takes to become a park ranger for the U.S. Forest Service.	**Evidence of reaching my goal:**
Steps **Date added:**	Action steps that will help meet my goal: 1. Meet with my advisor or counselor to discuss an ELO with a park ranger in the local region. 2. Develop an ELO proposal and submit to my advisor or counselor. 3. Coordinate a time to meet with a park ranger and develop a schedule to participate in my ELO. 4. Reflect on ELO experience in a blog and create an ELO Portfolio.	• ELO with a park ranger. • Learner Portfolio or presentation of experience of met competencies. **Date Achieved:**
Other supports I will need for my College and Career Goal: Transportation to the park ranger site.		
Set of apps/tools that could support my College and Career Goal: Note-taking, audio and video recording tools for recording my reflections; blog and portfolio tools; learning journal tool or app: (e.g., Notability, AudioNote, SeeSaw app (Learning Journal); Google Docs, Evernote, Dropbox, Drive, LiveBinders). These apps/technologies are available for iOS/Google Chrome, all platforms and devices. See Companion Website for other suggestions.		
Reflection on achieving my College and Career Goal 1: I was lucky to find a park ranger in a regional park close to my home who was willing to work with me. I got to follow her first to chronicle job responsibilities. Then we met to discuss all the skills needed to be a park ranger. I was glad I recorded audio notes and took pictures for my portfolio. I found participating in an ELO was very rewarding.		

Source: Personalize Learning, LLC.

Citizenship Goal

A Citizenship Goal serves as a way for a learner to contribute to his or her community, locally or globally (Table 4.13). Sometimes these experiences initiate an interest in a career choice, but in all cases, a Citizenship Goal contributes to a learner's understanding that a democracy thrives when you are an active citizen in the community.

Table 4.13   Example of PLP—Citizenship Goal

My Personal Learning Plan Name:		Progress
Citizenship Goal 1	I would like to be actively involved with the food drive for our local soup kitchen.	**Evidence of reaching my goal:**
Steps Date added:	Action steps that will help meet my goal: 1. Meet with advisor or counselor to discuss my goal and how I could get involved. 2. Meet with the food drive coordinator to schedule a time to work on food drive. 3. Collect nonperishable foods as needed for the local soup kitchen. 4. Work in organizing foods to send to soup kitchen.	Collect and organizing food for the soup kitchen on a regular basis. **Date Achieved:**
Other supports I will need for my Citizenship Goal: Transportation to food drive events.		
Set of apps/tools that could support my Citizenship Goal: blog and portfolio tools; learning journal tool or app (e.g., Notability, AudioNote, SeeSaw app (learning journal). These apps/technologies are available for iOS/Google Chrome, all platforms and devices.		
Reflection on achieving my Citizenship Goal 1: I always wanted to do something to give back to society. After I worked with the local soup kitchen and collected nonperishable foods, I decided to chronicle what happens at a soup kitchen in my blog. I felt lucky that people wanted to share their stories with pictures and videos of interviews. I realized that everyone has a story, and I can help share them.		

Source: Personalize Learning, LLC.

Personal Learning Plan (PLP) Goal Template

We included the PLP goal template on the Companion Website so it can be used for any goal that your learners may want to set. To get started, we included an activity for you to work with the learners on goal setting.

ACTIVITY 4.4
Goal Setting in a Personal Learning Plan

Take the LP and PLB that the learner created in Activity 4.3 to develop a learning goal with the learner. *(In the classroom setting, the learners would be developing the goal with the teacher.)*

1. Download the Table 4.14 Personal Learning Plan (PLP) Goal Template from the Companion Website and have the learner:

   a. Locate a strength or challenge under Access, Engage, or Express that could be developed into a goal.

   b. Indicate which one it is along with a goal statement starting with "I want to learn . . ."

   c. Describe the action steps to take to achieve this goal along with the date you set this goal.

   d. Describe what the evidence will be in reaching this goal.

   e. Provide a list of supports that may be needed for this goal.

   f. List the set of apps/tools that can support this goal.

   g. Indicate the date the goal is achieved and reflect on this achievement.

Table 4.14 Personal Learning Plan (PLP) Goal Template

My Personal Learning Plan Name:		Progress
-------- Goal 1		Evidence of reaching my goal: Date Achieved:
Steps Date added:	Action steps that will help meet my goal: 1. 2.	
Other supports I will need for my _____ Goal:		
Set of apps/tools that could support my _____ Goal:		
Reflection on achieving my _____ Goal 1:		

Source: Personalize Learning, LLC.

Conversation Starters

Discuss with your colleagues and principal:

1. The different ways that you can introduce the PLP and goal setting with your learners.

2. How and when PLP goals will be developed.

3. If there will be a specific time each week for learners to work on and review learning goals.

LP and PLP Examples

Many schools have created their own versions of PLPs. We want to share two that reflect different grade levels. These vignettes also provide some background on the process they took to develop their plans.

Liberty Elementary School, Riverside School District, California

In 2013, Riverside Unified School District (RUSD) was selected for a philanthropist grant for the implementation of Personalized Learning (PL), and Liberty Elementary was one of two elementary schools to begin the pilot process of implementing PL on a small scale. Liberty Elementary is a neighborhood school located in a low-income community with 93 percent of students receiving free or reduced-price lunches.

The pilot team created the Learner Profile and developed questions that started the conversations that allowed teachers to know *each* learner. The conversations became very emotional for teachers and learners because the cultural and religious beliefs students shared were very personal and opened our eyes to their lives at home. This was also the beginning of building lasting relationships between the teacher and child as the following story shows:

> *One third grader shared that she missed her grandfather and how they spent time together gardening back in Mexico where she cannot go back and see him again. He taught her how to garden and they would tend to the garden together almost every day. The teacher let the coordinator know, and they invited her to join the garden club. She is now very excited to be a part of the garden club.*

www.personalizelearning
.com/2016/03/validating-
learner-and-nurturing-their.html

The Personalized Learning Plan (PLP) is modified to adjust for student learning needs and how they will demonstrate mastery. We also see where they stand as readers, writers, and mathematicians. If the child cannot read, their plan includes goals for meeting reading standards. The PLP includes the teacher and learner working together as co-authors as they work on the plan, monitor progress on what the learner can and cannot do, and then reflect and show if the learner mastered competencies.

Then the learner's profile is updated to show changes or add new areas to their plans. The learner has a voice and choice on knowing who he or she is as a learner.

To read more of this story with examples of the LP and PLP, please visit our website.

Mount Abraham Union Middle/High School, Bristol, Vermont

Caroline Patrie, a longtime Personalized Learning Coordinator for Mount Abraham Union Middle/High School and currently the Addison Northeast Supervisory Union (ANESU) Innovation Coach shared the history of the school's Personal Learning Plans.

Mount Abraham Union Middle/High School began their journey with Personal Learning Plans (PLPs) over 15 years ago. Courses were developed in seventh and eighth grades to begin the Making Action Plans (MAPs) process, in which learners were asked to describe themselves by answering the question, "Who Am I?" Learners were assigned an advisor for 2 years in seventh and eighth grades, meeting 10 minutes a day with the same advisor. In high school, each learner was assigned an advisor for 4 years, and they met for 20 minutes a day. With the advent of Vermont's Act 77, the Flexible Pathways to Graduation legislation, the PLP gained more traction, and all seventh and ninth graders needed to have an active PLP in place by November 2015.

Currently, we use Google Sites to create a template for each class that contains a place to house the PLP and for learners to collect evidence of their learning to meet their graduation requirements, known as the Mount Abraham Competencies. The PLP section allows learners to update their evidence, reflections, and goals. The responsibility of supporting learners falls on the advisors. The school counselors, innovation coach for the supervisory union, and the administration have worked together to support the advisors with a demo site for each class, which provides examples for the learners to see how they can create evidence in each of the sections.

Seventh Grade:

We start with the Who Am I? components because middle school learners LOVE to talk about themselves. We ask them to tell about their hobbies, family histories, strengths, and challenges. What they choose to tell you reveals a great deal about who they are. We encourage them to explore new tools to demonstrate this information. It does not always have to be in a paragraph form; it can include collage-creating software, music in the background, creative fonts—all middle school gold.

Ninth Grade:

We always go back to the Who Am I? components to start the high school years. We provide time for the learners to update, encouraging them to go deeper into their stories, or to explain why characteristics of themselves have shifted. Working in the 4-Year Plan is key at this point. Even if the learners do not know what their goals are after high school, collaborating to plan how they want to go about their learning to get their graduation requirements is a fantastic conversation. We revisit it each year and use this to help learners set short- and long-term goals.

An example of a PLP from Mount Abraham Union Middle/High School can be located on the Companion Website under this chapter heading.

"To inspire meaningful change, you must make a connection to the heart before you can make a connection to the mind." — George Couros (2015)

Partnership in Learning by Discovering the Learner

As learners share the stories of how they learn with their teacher, they become partners in learning. Reflecting on the LP opens the door to have regular conversations between the teacher and learners about their learning. The teacher and learners then can refer to their LPs to develop a PLB with the tools, apps, resources, strategies, and skills to support their learning. The PLP continues the conversation to help learners articulate their goals, action steps to achieve those goals, and how they will measure progress.

Teachers realized how helpful the LP is in understanding how learners learn best and how the PLP helps them develop and set goals. Then they asked us how to personalize learning for a whole class or multiple classes. Chapter 5 shares how you can use what you learned in this and preceding chapters to create a Class Learning Snapshot to design instruction that meets the needs of all learners in your class or classes.

www.personalizelearning
.com/2014/11/changing-
perceptions-every-child-learner.
html

Build the Common Language

Add the common language to the list that you started from the previous chapters or to the Padlet on the Companion Website.

- What conversations are you having now as your learners are setting goals and action steps in their PLPs?
- What common language in this chapter enhances your understanding of the UDL lens of Access, Engage, and Express.

Review: Write a reflection on what you learned about understanding learners and how you can build relationships with your learners.

Learn: By using this three-step process, what did you learn about your learners that you did not know before?

Apply: What goals and action steps will you take to use the Learner Profile, Personal Learning Backpack, and Personal Learning Plan in your practice?

5

Personalize Learning for a Whole Class

How do I personalize learning for all the learners in my class(es)?

Now that you know how to understand how your learners learn best, you are probably wondering how to take the information you learned to design instruction for an entire class. You can universally design your lessons to include tools and instructional methods that teach the maximum number of learners by anticipating just four learners. The first part of this process is called the Class Learning Snapshot (CLS). The take-aways for this chapter include how to create a CLS by using the Learner Profiles (LPs) of four diverse learners and how to build a Class Learning Toolkit (CLT) with the tools, apps, resources, and instructional methods to teach the maximum number of learners in your class (see Figure 5.1).

CLASS LEARNING SNAPSHOT (CLS)

The **Class Learning Snapshot (CLS)** helps teachers universally design their instructional methods and materials based on the learners who are in their class or classes. The CLS includes the strengths and challenges that your learners have in accessing information, engaging with content, and expressing what they know, along with their interests, aspirations, and

| Figure 5.1 | The Class Learning Snapshot and Class Learning Toolkit Process |

Class Learning Snapshot
- Anticipate the strengths, interests, talents, and challenges of four diverse learners.

Preferences and Needs
- Indicate how these four learners need or prefer to access, engage, and express.

Class Learning Toolkit
- Choose tools, resources, and methods to instruct the maximum number of learners.

Source: Personalize Learning, LLC.

passions. Next, you include what they prefer and need to learn as it relates to Access, Engage, and Express.

Choosing Four Learners

We recommend starting with four diverse learners in your class. Neuroscience explains that when you design instruction, you should base it on the learners that you have at the ends of the learning spectrum and not what you believe is the average learner. There are no average learners in your class (Rose, 2013).

Teachers can develop a CLS that anticipates four learners' strengths, interests, talents, and challenges in accessing information, engaging with content, and expressing what they know and understand. If you have multiple classes, you can choose four diverse learners from one of your classes that you have or will have.

> *"If you design those learning environments around average, odds are you've designed them for nobody. So no wonder we have a problem. We've created learning environments that because they are designed on average cannot possibly do what we expected them to do, which is nurture individual potential." — The Myth of Average: Todd Rose at TEDxSonoma County, 2013*

Consider This!

The learning spectrum is about the learners who have cognitive or learning challenges at one end of the spectrum to the other end with self-directed, independent learners. The ends or extremes of the learning spectrum will guide how you can universally design your instruction to meet the needs of most of the learners in your class or classes rather than for the needs of the average learner who does not exist.

Preferences and Needs

Next, you include what the four learners prefer and need to learn as it relates to how they access, engage, and express. One learner may not be able to decode words so that learner may need to use a text-to-speech tool for reading. Another learner may share that he or she has trouble organizing and prefers to use graphic organizers to help organize ideas. If you have had your four learners complete the LPs from Chapter 4, the information they included about themselves as learners can be used for the CLS with any additional information that you would like to include about these four learners.

In the example CLS in Table 5.1, we used each learner's initials instead of names to provide anonymity. We recommend that you may want to do the same or use another way to provide anonymity.

As we discussed earlier, engagement is the affective side of learning: what learners are interested in, have identified as talents, or what they aspire to be. This can be the hook. As you develop the CLS, you can also keep track of learners' aspirations, talents, interests, and passions. These can help you develop specific assignments with voice and choice. For example, learners who are artistic can draw posters to demonstrate understanding of a concept instead of writing an essay.

You will also want to consider *why* your learners will want to engage with the content. Learners want to learn more about something they are interested in. Someone who aspires to be an architect will want to do research about what architecture means and what skills are necessary so that they are prepared for college. If learners are given options to pursue their interests for projects, they want to learn more and show what they found out. If instruction taps into their talents, they are more motivated to use their talents to demonstrate what they know.

In Activity 5.1, you will create a CLS of *four* diverse learners' strengths, interests, challenges, preferences, and needs using their initials instead of their names, such as OB, JT, SM, and JR. Some teachers use code names such as Learner 1, Learner 2, and so forth. These four learners need to be from a single class who come from the ends of the learning spectrum.

Table 5.1   Example of a Class Learning Snapshot (CLS)

Class Learning Snapshot (CLS)			
Learners	**Strengths, Talents, and Interests**	**Challenges**	**Preferences and Needs**
OB	• Works well with others • Great at photography • Challenges himself to learn more	• Has anxiety about taking tests • Trouble organizing • Cannot sit still • English is a second language	**Access:** prefers folder system for digital files; needs translator **Engage:** prefers to collect or create images for group projects **Express:** needs to present with visuals
JT	• Good sense of humor • Very artistic • Excellent social skills	• Does not understand what he reads • Low vocabulary skills • Trouble putting thoughts to paper • Jokes around	**Access:** prefers using digital files for instructional materials and books, needs appropriate reading level, prefers games and videos **Engage:** prefers to lead group activities, learns with video and music **Express:** needs to create a game, illustrate concept, or act in video
SM	• Strong reader • Very creative • Works well with others	• Needs things to be perfect • Anxious speaking in front of others • Uncomfortable asking for help • Cannot visualize content	**Access:** prefers note-taking and summarizing reading for understanding **Engage:** needs to keep a reflective journal and illustrate story **Express:** prefers to write a blog and draw pictures
JR	• Asks for help when working on tasks • Really focuses on tasks when working • Knows how to use and choose technology for tasks	• Difficulty organizing ideas • Not able to write descriptively • Trouble working with others • Does not have a lot of friends	**Access:** needs visuals for textbooks and instructional materials, templates or graphic organizers for writing **Engage:** prefers to design and build models; needs one-on-one with teacher for help with tasks **Express:** prefers to present with video, sound, audio notes, and graphics

Source: Personalize Learning, LLC.

ACTIVITY 5.1
Class Learning Snapshot

You can download the Table 5.2 CLS template from the Companion Website. Then review and summarize the LPs of the four learners and what they wrote for their strengths, challenges, interests, preferences, and needs to complete this CLS.

1. Indicate each learner's strengths, interests, talents, and challenges in how they Access (and process) information, Engage with content, and Express what they know and understand. Using the Universal Design for Learning (UDL) lens of Access, Engage, and Express will give you a better picture of who they are as learners.

2. Complete the CLS by including their preferences and needs as it relates to Access, Engage, and Express.

Be sure to include ways that might help you to select the best pedagogical strategies to help learners understand their own learning preferences so they can better access and engage with content and express what they are learning or have learned.

Table 5.2   Class Learning Snapshot Template

Class Learning Snapshot (CLS)			
Learners	**Strengths, Talents, and Interests**	**Challenges**	**Preferences and Needs**
	• •	• •	Access: Engage: Express:
	• •	• •	Access: Engage: Express:
	• •	• •	Access: Engage: Express:
	• •	• •	Access: Engage: Express:

Source: Personalize Learning, LLC.

To take this a step further, choose one of your learners and plan a short activity to demonstrate how you will address how that person learns as a learner.

Conversation Starters

After adding your four learners and their strengths, interests, challenges, preferences, and needs, review what you wrote and write a reflection summarizing how these four learners encompass the diversity of all the learners in your class or classes.

- How does the CLS help you understand how your learners learn? How do they need to access information, engage with content, and express what they know and understand?
- Did you learn something new about your learners you did not know before doing the CLS?
- Does one learner stand out to you? Why? How might you change your instructional strategies after what you found out about this learner?

CLASS LEARNING TOOLKIT (CLT)

The **Class Learning Toolkit (CLT)** includes the tools, apps, resources, and instructional strategies that you will use to engage your learners in a lesson. In addition, you will include the learning strategies and skills your four learners need. This is determined from the CLS you created.

Tools, Apps, and Resources

The tools, apps, and resources you can use in your CLT initially will be based on what your four diverse learners will need to access and engage with the content and to express what they know and understand. For each lesson, you can refer back to your four diverse learners in the CLS when selecting additional tools to support your instruction so that all of your learners will understand and be engaged with the content or concepts. For example, if you have a CLS where the learners may need to have a simulation to understand a concept, then the simulation would be a part of your CLT that would be accessible to all of your learners. When you are creating the CLT, you should also indicate the learning strategies and skills your learners may need to have to effectively use the CLT.

In Table 5.3, the first column provides some tools and apps that might support four diverse learners in 1:1 tablet, laptop, or Chromebook environments. Additional apps can be found on the Companion Website for Chapter 4 under the Personal Learning Backpack. The second column provides ideas for instructional methods the teachers could implement with the corresponding tool/app. The third column lists the learning strategies and skills that learners will acquire before that tool/app and instructional method will be effective.

Table 5.3 Example Tools/Apps, Instructional Methods, and Learning Strategies and Skills

Tools/Apps	Instructional Methods	Learning Strategies and Skills
Access		
Popplet (iPhone, iPad, and iPod touch)	Teacher can illustrate a sequence of steps, create a storyboard, or use it for brainstorming with a class.	Learners can organize ideas for writing in a project or to break down tasks.
Voice Dream Reader (iPhone, iPad, and iPod touch, Android)	Teacher can use embedded sticky notes, highlighting, and dictionary to demonstrate comprehension strategies.	Learners can use text-to-speech and customized font options to access books and other digital materials independently or use it as a translator.
Read & Write (Chrome extension, Mac or PC, iOS, Android—all devices/platforms)	Teacher can engage all learners with audio and create study guides with the class using research tools.	Learners with embedded text-to-speech and research tools can use this to read articles online independently and take notes by highlighting.
Engage		
Notability (iPhone, iPad, and iPod Touch)	Teacher can use this to illustrate and record audio notes. Also used to "flip" the classroom: all learners view the video, audio, and lecture before coming to class and then discuss what they learned in class.	Learners can use this to take notes, organize information, and include audio, photos, web clips, and drawings of concepts and ideas.
Google Apps for Education (GAFE) (all devices/platforms)	Teacher organizes and models lessons and project materials, graphics, and video in a folder/file management system.	Learners can use Google Drive to collaborate on an activity in groups or with partners. Learners can use it to organize lesson and project resources, assignments, graphics, video, and audio files in a folder/file management system.
Express		
Educreations (iPad)	Teacher introduces lesson by importing images, adding illustrations, and recording voice that includes step-by-step instructions in lesson website.	Learners incorporate text, drawings, and video, along with audio comments to respond to assessment questions.
Book Creator (iPad and Android)	Teacher models apps and tools by creating book with the class.	Learners incorporate their own photos and drawings in original stories.
Explain Everything (EE) (iPhone, iPad, iPod touch, and Android)	Teacher includes images and video with narration to introduce a new concept and adds to lesson website. This app offers a multisensory and media approach to representation, engagement, and expression for teacher and learner.	Learners collaborate in a group to create an EE doc to respond to lesson question. She or he shares doc that includes original drawings and narration with teacher.

Source: Personalize Learning, LLC.

Instructional Methods, Learning Strategies, and Skills

After teachers identify the tools, apps, and resources similar to Table 5.3, they can use Table 5.4 to create a CLT based on the four learners from the CLS.

Table 5.4   Example Class Learning Toolkit

Class Learning Toolkit (CLT)			
Learners	Tools, Apps, and Resources	Instructional Methods	Learning Strategies and Skills
OB	Folder/file management system available (e.g., Dropbox, Google Drive); translators, both app and online	Teacher models a folder and file management system at teacher station for whole class. Teacher or instructional coach demonstrates how to use translators for small group.	OB works with partner who can help him organize digital folders and files including captured images. OB uses a translator for books, materials, and online resources.
JT	Text-to-speech tool in iOS devices (e.g., Voice Dream Reader); Minecraft	Teacher or instructional coach demonstrates text-to-speech tool for reading comprehension with small group.	JT uses his headphones or earplugs and goes to a quiet area to read using the text-to-speech program. JT reads Minecraft series to learn how to create online world.
SM	Note-taking tool with audio features (e.g., Notability, Audio Note)	Teacher reviews note-taking skills and the use of audio and sketch features.	SM works with partner to help her take notes using a note-taking app and uses the audio feature to play back for understanding.
JR	Graphic organizer (e.g., Popplet, Tools4Students, and LucidChart for Education)	Teacher uses storyboarding using a graphic organizer (e.g., Popplet) to demonstrate sequencing in a story.	JR brainstorms order of story using Popplet or drawing with markers on whiteboard with others in his group.
Other Instructional Notes: Use of an interactive whiteboard or a LCD projector to project instruction and demonstration of tools for the class is necessary.			

Source: Personalize Learning, LLC.

Table 5.4 includes specific tools, apps, or resources that can support the learning for each of your four learners. Using these tools will help meet the needs of other learners in your class who also benefit from the instructional methods listed here. The teacher can identify the learning strategies for each learner and may want to consult one-on-one with the learners to guide them in the use of these tools, apps, and resources.

Review UDL Guidelines

Before you create the CLT, we suggest that you review the UDL Guidelines developed by the Center for Applied Special Technology (CAST) to assist teachers in planning universally designed lessons that reduce barriers to learning as well as optimize levels of challenge and support to meet the needs of all learners from the start. CAST developed an interactive website for the nine UDL Guidelines along with specific Checkpoints for each guideline that offer examples of tools and resources to guide implementation along with the research evidence for each Checkpoint (www.udlcenter.org/aboutudl/udlguidelines).

To get you started, we created an activity with templates around the UDL Solutions and Strategies on the Companion Website to help you explore the UDL Guidelines and Checkpoints in relation to Access, Engage, and Express. They include tools and apps that can support your instructional methods, materials, and assessment.

ACTIVITY 5.2
Class Learning Toolkit (CLT)

Use the template in Table 5.5 that is available on the Companion Website to complete the CLT. Refer to your CLS as you build it.

1. Use the initials of the four learners you indicated in the CLS.

2. Under Tools, Apps, and Resources, indicate what each of these four learners will need to support his or her ability to access information, engage with the content, and express what he or she knows and understands. Include any tools, apps, or resources you will need to support your instruction.

3. Describe under Instructional Methods how you will use the tool, app, or resource with your class. Keep in mind that tools, apps, and resources can be added or changed based on the lesson that is being taught.

4. For Learning Strategies and Skills, indicate the strategies and skills your four learners will need and how they will use these tools, apps, and resources. If skills need to be taught, then indicate who will work with that learner or how the learner can acquire those skills independently.

5. Under Other Instructional Notes, describe any other tool, app, or resource that may be needed to instruct the learners effectively or could be used by your learners to support their learning.

Table 5.5   Class Learning Toolkit Template

Class Learning Toolkit (CLT)			
Learners	Tools, Apps, and Resources	Instructional Methods	Learning Strategies and Skills
Other Instructional Notes:			

Source: Personalize Learning, LLC.

Conversation Starters

- How will you use the CLT in your daily practice?
- What tools, apps, and resources do you see as most effective with the maximum number of learners in your class?
- Are there any challenges or barriers that some of your learners have that could affect their learning?

After you complete your CLT, you will be able to gather the resources and strategies for the four learners that you can then apply to your entire class. When you consider trying to find additional tools, apps, and resources for other learners in your class(es), we recommend that you review the UDL Guidelines and resources mentioned before we introduced the CLT.

Using the CLS and the CLT, Chapter 6 will introduce you to the UDL Lesson Review Process to understand how to determine the methods, materials, and assessments to universally design your lessons. This is followed by the two-part UDL Lesson Design that provides guidance about how to frame and design lessons for all learners in your daily practice.

Build the Common Language

 Add the common language to the list that you started from the previous chapters.

- Now that you created a CLS and CLT, how does this connect with the common language about the LP and PLB?
- If other colleagues are creating a CLS, have you collaborated on the instructional methods and tools that you will include in your CLT?

 Review: Reflect on the CLS and how it may affect your decision on instructional methods and materials.

Learn: What new ideas did you learn that could be applied in your daily practice?

Apply: Describe what your action steps will be in using the CLS/CLT process.

6

Lesson Design With All Learners in Mind

How do I develop lessons that meet the needs of all the learners in my class?

The challenge each day in the classroom is how you will teach every learner every day. The Class Learning Snapshot (CLS) and Class Learning Toolkit (CLT) that you created in Chapter 5 will help you design your lessons with the process that we will show you in this chapter.

Before you get started with designing a lesson, let's take a closer look at a lesson review process that will help you decide on the methods, materials, and assessments you will use in any lesson. Your takeaways in this chapter will be understanding the Universal Design for Learning (UDL) Lesson Review Process by applying it to your own lesson, knowing how to create a vocabulary activity with visuals, and designing a lesson with all learners in mind.

> **Consider This!**
>
> When teachers understand who their learners are and how they learn, then teachers will be able to better decide on the instructional methods and materials for their lessons.

FOUR-STEP UDL LESSON REVIEW PROCESS

When reviewing a lesson, apply the UDL Lesson Review Process in Figure 6.1 to decide on the methods, materials, and assessments that can support the learners found in your CLS. Once you use this process, apply it in your daily lessons and make it a part of your teaching practice. This process will help you understand what the four learners from your CLS are required to do with the methods, materials, and assessments and what possible barriers there may be for them. In the end, arriving at what the UDL Solutions and Strategies will be for these learners will help you universally design your lessons for the whole class.

Figure 6.1   Four-Step UDL Lesson Review Process

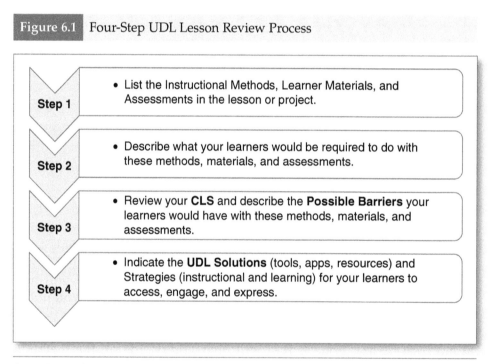

Step 1
- List the Instructional Methods, Learner Materials, and Assessments in the lesson or project.

Step 2
- Describe what your learners would be required to do with these methods, materials, and assessments.

Step 3
- Review your **CLS** and describe the **Possible Barriers** your learners would have with these methods, materials, and assessments.

Step 4
- Indicate the **UDL Solutions** (tools, apps, resources) and Strategies (instructional and learning) for your learners to access, engage, and express.

Source: Personalize Learning, LLC.

Table 6.1 shows an example of a sixth-grade standards-based literature lesson where we applied the four-step UDL Lesson Review Process. We are using the book *Roll of Thunder, Hear My Cry* by Mildred D. Taylor (1976) to demonstrate this process because middle schoolers can relate to the concepts of family and pride.

Table 6.1 UDL Lesson Review Process Example

Methods, Materials, and Assessments

Sixth-Grade Literature Lesson on *Roll of Thunder, Hear My Cry* by Mildred D. Taylor

Instructional Methods, Materials, and Assessments	Requires Learners to	Possible Barriers	UDL Solutions and Strategies
Learners learn content by independently reading the book, *Roll of Thunder, Hear My Cry* **by Mildred D. Taylor.**	Read independently Comprehend content Read at **Lexile score** 920, which ranges from 6th through 8th grade levels	JT does not understand what he reads. SM cannot visualize content. OB is a second language learner.	Provide learners with a variety of media and formats Pair with a good reader Provide a tool or app that offers translation
During classroom lecture, the teacher summarizes the story and the theme of discrimination.	Be able to hear and understand audio lectures and the term *discrimination*	JT has low vocabulary skills. OB cannot sit still. JR has difficulty organizing ideas.	Provide written or multimedia options of summary Highlight/speak difficult words with definitions
During whole-group instruction, the teacher shows 20 minutes of YouTube video of *Roll of Thunder, Hear My Cry** **and follows with class discussion.**	Summarize notes Focus on video Be able to hear and see video Participate in discussion Defend position on discrimination	SM is anxious speaking front of others. JR has trouble working with others. OB cannot sit still and is a second language learner.	Embed video on class website so learners can watch later Include subtitles for ELL learners Provide learning spaces that offer quiet and privacy Encourage learners to work in pairs to review and discuss video
Learners complete worksheets on how *Roll of Thunder, Hear My Cry* **is about racism and the Depression for class work.**	Read directions Write descriptively Do research on racism during the Depression	OB is a second language learner. JT is not able to understand written direction. SM is uncomfortable asking for help.	Provide a digital file Provide a tool or app that offers translation and text-to-speech Include a tool or app that includes audio notes and sketching
Learners are given a summative assessment that includes multiple choice and short answers.	Answer questions succinctly Prioritize what to do next Complete assessment on time	JT has trouble putting thoughts to paper. JR is not able to write descriptively. SM needs things to be perfect. OB has anxiety about taking tests.	Provide a digital file Provide a speech-to-text tool or a tool that has audio notes Walk through summative assessment with whole class

*YouTube video of movie: https://youtu.be/U2ZbrNMQtfo

Source: Personalize Learning, LLC.

In this lesson example, we discover that traditional instructional methods of presenting information orally were included in this lesson. The lesson materials were in hard copy for the book and handout but included a video along with a class discussion. The summative assessment was in the form of a hard copy and was not accessible for these learners, so we provided a digital file alongside a text-to-speech tool. These represent just a few examples of UDL Solutions and Strategies for this lesson. We used the CLS example from Chapter 5 and included the challenges these four learners would have with the methods, materials, and assessments. To apply this to a lesson of your own, download the PDF form of the UDL Lesson Review Process Template from the Companion Website (Table 6.2).

Table 6.2   UDL Lesson Review Process Template

Instructional Methods, Materials, and Assessments	Requires Learners to	Possible Barriers	UDL Solutions and Strategies

Source: Personalize Learning, LLC.

ACTIVITY 6.1
UDL Lesson Review Process

Step 1: List the Instructional Methods,
Learner Materials, and Assessments in the lesson or project.

Every lesson includes a set of instructional methods that may include an oral presentation, a PowerPoint presentation, a video, a demonstration, a simulation, and modeling. Lesson materials that are prepared for the learners often include hard copies of handouts and books, hands-on materials in conjunction with directions—just to name a few. Assessments can come in the form of oral checks for understanding, quizzes, tests, oral presentations, self-reflections, and portfolios. Each of these should be listed when initially using this process to review the lesson.

Step 2: Describe what your learners would be
required to do with these methods, materials, and assessments.

What are learners required to do with each instructional method, set of materials, and assessment? This may be something you have not thought about before, but it needs to be described here so you can think more deeply about the methods, materials, and assessments you have used in a lesson.

Step 3: Review your CLS and describe the possible barriers your
learners would have with these methods, materials, and assessments.

Take the four learners' challenges, preferences, and needs from your CLS and describe what possible barriers and missed opportunities could be incurred with what is required that they do with the current methods, materials, and assessments in the lesson.

Step 4: Indicate the UDL Solutions (tools, apps, and resources)
and Strategies (instructional and learning) you could use with
the whole class to access, engage, and express.

Review the possible barriers your learners from your CLS would have and then decide which UDL Solutions and Strategies to provide for the class. Take a close look at your four learners' strengths, preferences, and needs because these could be part of the UDL Solutions. Consider what instructional methods and tools you may want to use in your CLT based on these barriers. Include any learning strategies or skills that your learners may need to use any tool or app effectively. Examples of UDL Solutions and Strategies can be located next to help you decide what solutions and strategies would be most effective for most of your learners in your class. Describe how your learners will access information and materials in the lesson, engage with the content, and express what they know and understand.

UDL Solutions and Strategies

Every learner in your class is unique and different from every other learner. The UDL Solutions and Strategies in Table 6.3 are adapted from Maryland Learning Links to guide teachers in universally designing instruction to reduce the barriers to the curriculum and to maximize the learning for all learners. We have indicated how some of these solutions and strategies can provide voice and choice to the learner in the design of a lesson.

Table 6.3	Examples of UDL Solutions and Strategies

Access	• Provide multiple examples • Highlight important information • Present content using multiple media and formats • Build or activate background knowledge • Offer print and digital graphic organizers (Choice) • Provide hard copy or digital file of text or materials (Choice) • Provide text-to-speech tools or translators (Choice) • Provide relevant web resources with multiple formats for information (magazine, primary source photos, speeches, etc.) (Choice)
Engage	• Offer choices of content and tools (Choice) • Provide adjustable levels of challenge (Choice) • Allow learners to choose from a variety of ways to engage with content (Choice) • Use flexible grouping (Choice) • Allow learners to work individually or in groups (Choice) • Offer opportunities to publish, display, and present final products (school website, student assembly, back-to-school night, local library, etc.) (Choice) • Provide checklists for learners to monitor progress toward completion • Provide opportunities for learners to articulate their learning targets (Voice)
Express	• Model skills in a variety of ways • Provide learners with opportunities to practice with scaffolds and supports (Choice) • Provide corrective feedback • Allow alternatives for learners to express or demonstrate their learning (Voice and Choice) • Provide options for creating projects, written reports, multimedia, interviews, etc. (Choice) • Provide specific examples to guide your learners' learning • Conference with learners throughout the learning process (Voice) • Provide or co-design with your learners a rubric that outlines expectations (Voice)

Source: Adapted from Maryland Learning Links, 2015. Retrieved from https://marylandlearninglinks.org/resource/instructional-methods/

Extended resources can be located in the UDL Guidelines for specific tools and strategies (http://www.udlcenter.org/aboutudl/udlguidelines)

Conversation Starters

- What did you learn about your methods, materials, and assessments and the possible barriers they may have with your learners?
- What new UDL Solutions and Strategies did you discover in the process of reviewing your learners' strengths, preferences, and needs?
- How did your instructional strategies change based on who your learners were in the CLS?

LESSON DESIGN

When you begin dipping your toes into personalized learning, you will be giving more voice and choice in your lessons. Design your lesson so that your learners can access and be engaged with the content, ask questions, explore and practice with supports, and show mastery of their learning targets in the way they best express what they know.

Part 1—Frame the Lesson

The Lesson Design With All Learners in Mind has been developed in two parts. In Part 1, you are framing your lesson with the goal, objectives, standards, learning targets, assessment plan, and vocabulary (Table 6.4). When creating each element in this part, consider these questions to help you frame the lesson. We are sharing some ideas for a lesson from *Roll of Thunder, Hear My Cry* for the lesson example. We also will be going deeper with some of these elements in the next chapter.

Table 6.4   Part 1—Frame the Lesson

Lesson	Questions to Consider	Lesson Example
Goal	What is the goal of the lesson? What is the driving question?	The goal is to understand the theme of family and struggle. "How does being a family help the Logans survive discrimination?"
Objectives	What will your learners learn and be able to do or demonstrate? How will they apply this new knowledge?	Learners will write about one event that involved how the Logan family fought racism and then share what family or prejudice means to them.
Standards and Learning Targets	What are the standards that you will use in this lesson? What are the learning targets? How will you give each learner voice and choice with the learning targets?	Reading: Literature (RL) Standard 2: Determine a theme or central idea of a text and how it is conveyed through particular details; provide a summary of the text distinct from personal opinions or judgments. Give learners voice by having them articulate the learning targets in their own words. Give learners choices by having them state how they will meet the learner targets.
Assessment Plan	Based on your lesson review, • What formative assessments will you use in this lesson to check for understanding and self-reflection? • What ways will learners have to demonstrate mastery of their learning targets?	Learners can reflect on their learning as they learn. They can write or record in journals as they read about what happens with Cassie and her family. Consider the ways that each learner can demonstrate mastery of learning by understanding how he or she can best express what they know.
Vocabulary: New and Review	How will you present new and review vocabulary with learners using multiple representations so that every learner will understand?	Vocabulary is presented using different representations (see Activity 6.2) so that each learner can access the words through pictures and audio means. Learners will speak, understand, and apply vocabulary throughout the lesson.

Source: Personalize Learning, LLC.

Personalizing learning means reducing barriers to the curriculum, including the words used. When learners have difficulty knowing what a word means or why it is being used, it can keep them from meeting a learning goal or mastering a concept.

Vocabulary: New and Review

To encourage learning of a topic or concept, learners need to understand the vocabulary so that they can make connections to the content. Teachers can help learners develop a strong working vocabulary by encouraging a curiosity about the meaning and use of unfamiliar words. Vocabulary falls into four categories:

1. Listening: the words we understand when we hear them

2. Speaking: the words we use when talking

3. Reading: the words we understand when we read

4. Writing: the words we use when writing

> **Promote learner ownership by having learners**
>
> - work in pairs to acquire the visuals, audio, or video of the vocabulary to share with the entire class and then place in a shared folder; and
> - create a shared site where this vocabulary can be accessed.

To support all the learners in your class, vocabulary words need to be introduced using multiple representations of the word (Table 6.5). Consider using these:

- Visuals or photos of the word
- Links to a website that can illustrate the word
- Audio pronunciation of the word
- Having the learner pronounce the word
- Video links to provide understanding of the concept or word
- Flash cards or trading cards

Table 6.5   Example of Vocabulary Activity for *Roll of Thunder, Hear My Cry*

Word	Definition	Image	Representation
Sharecropping *(include audio pronunciation and have learner pronounce the word)*	A system of agriculture in which a landowner allows a tenant to use the land in return for a share of the crops produced on the tenant's portion of land. (Wikipedia)	 Black female sharecropper picking cotton (1939). (Wikipedia)	Sharecropping videos: http://www .history.com/topics/ black-history/ sharecropping/ videos
Sentence Meaning: After the Civil War, sharecropping was common across the cotton-planting South.			
Mercantile *(include audio pronunciation and have learner pronounce the word)*	Of or relating to the business of buying and selling products to earn money. (Merriam-Webster.com)	 Virgelle Mercantile.jpg (Wikipedia)	Mercantile Video: https://www .youtube.com/ watch?v=APSo3-IreuY
Sentence Meaning: We walked to the local mercantile to buy supplies.			

Source: Personalize Learning, LLC.

ACTIVITY 6.2
Vocabulary With Visuals

1. Download the Vocabulary With Visuals Activity Template from the Companion Website. *[Remember the link and passcode to the Companion Website are located in the Introduction.]*

2. In the first column, Word, identify and discuss with your learners the words that may be unfamiliar with them from a lesson you are planning. Add an audio pronunciation of the word or a link to the pronunciation beneath the word.

3. In the second column, Definition, have your learners add the definition and where they located it.

4. In the third column, Image, have your learners include an image of the word.

5. In the fourth column, Representation, have your learners include a video and/or simulation.

6. In the Sentence Meaning, have your learners use this word in a sentence.

Use the template in Table 6.6 to have your learners build a "vocabulary with visuals" bank for your lessons that can be shared. Have your learners present the vocabulary to the class.

Table 6.6   Vocabulary Activity Template

Word	Definition	Image	Representation
Sentence Meaning:			
Sentence Meaning:			

Source: Personalize Learning, LLC.

 Conversation Starters

- How did this vocabulary activity support my learners?
- What did your learners say about this activity?
- Are the vocabulary and symbols clear to all learners?

ACTIVITY 6.3
Part 1—Framing Your Lesson

- Download the template Part 1—Framing Your Lesson (Table 6.7) from the Companion Website.
- Take a lesson you currently do and complete the template below using the guiding questions from Table 6.4.

Table 6.7	Part 1—Framing Your Lesson
Lesson	
Goal	
Objectives	
Standards and Learning Targets	
Assessment Plan	
Vocabulary: New and Review	

Source: Personalize Learning, LLC.

Part 2—Lesson Design

In Part 2, you are designing your lesson with the lesson kickoff followed by the lesson exploration, practice, and check for understanding. Next, you will extend the lesson and provide opportunities for independent practice so that learners can dive deeper in their understanding and demonstrate mastery of their learning targets. Lesson Design (Table 6.8) was created to be more generic without reference to any lesson so it is more of a guide for you. Throughout the lesson design process, you can refer to the UDL Strategies and Solutions mentioned earlier in this chapter.

Lesson Elements	Questions to Consider	UDL Strategies and Solutions
Lesson Kickoff and Engagement	How will you engage your learners in the lesson? How will you activate prior knowledge and generate questions?	**Access:** Activate prior knowledge and illustrate key concepts using graphics, photos, simulations, or video with close captions. **Engage:** Recruit learners' interests or talents, and generate questions from learners.
Lesson Exploration and Guided Practice	How will you give your learners access to the content of the lesson? What alternatives to language-based learning will you provide? What options will you give to provide guided practice? What challenges and supports will you build into your lesson to encourage exploration?	**Access:** Represent information in different ways for your learners to have access to the content. **Engage:** Offer various levels of challenge and support. **Express:** Offer options to practice, problem solve, and question.
Check for Understanding and Create Understanding (Formative Assessment)	How will you check for understanding and create understanding? (Assessment FOR learning) How will you give your learners voice and choice so that they can reflect on their learning and monitor their own progress? (Assessment AS Learning)	**Access:** Show key concepts through different mediums; respond to any questions for clarification. **Engage:** Offer opportunities for self-reflection and evaluation to create understanding. **Express:** Provide options for learners to express what they know and to discuss and monitor progress in their learning.
Response to Learning	Based on outcomes during formative assessment, create groups • to direct remediation for specific need of learners • to offer opportunities to expand the learning for learners that need challenges	
Lesson Expansion and Independent Practice	How will you expand the lesson for your learners to review, question, learn, and apply? How will you give learners choices in their independent practice based on their strengths, talents, interests, or needs? How will you scaffold the practice for learners to learn at their own paces and to achieve independence?	**Access:** Offer content in flexible ways so that all learners access information for independent practice. **Engage:** Offer learners individual choices based on their preferences, needs, or interests. **Express:** Provide options for learners to extend practice and reflect on what they learned in the way they prefer or need to express.
Indicate Mastery with Voice and Choice (Assessment)	How will your learners demonstrate mastery of their learning targets? How will they have voice and choice in demonstrating mastery?	**Access:** Provide learners a choice in how they will access the assessments. **Engage:** Offer choices in the levels of challenge as to engage each learner. **Express:** Offer learners choices in how they can respond in the assessment based on the ways they best express what they know and understand.
Reflection	Did all your learners understand the big idea and achieve the outcomes? What instructional strategies worked and did not work?	

Source: Personalize Learning, LLC.

ACTIVITY 6.4
Part 2—Your Lesson Design

1. Download Part 2—Your Lesson Design Template from the Companion Website (Table 6.9)

2. Outline the instructional methods and materials that you will use for each element of the lesson. Refer to the guiding questions from Table 6.8.

3. Make notes on how you will apply the UDL lens of Access, Engage, and Express in deciding the UDL Strategies and Solutions found earlier in this chapter.

Table 6.9 Part 2—Your Lesson Design Template

Lesson Elements	Instructional Methods and Materials	UDL Strategies and Solutions
Lesson Kickoff and Engagement		Access: Engage:
Lesson Exploration and Guided Practice		Access: Engage: Express:
Check for Understanding and Create Understanding (Formative Assessment)	(Assessment FOR learning) (Assessment AS Learning)	Access: Engage: Express:
Response to Learning	Based on outcomes during formative assessment, create groups . . .	
Lesson Expansion and Independent Practice		Access: Engage: Express:
Indicate Mastery with Voice and Choice (Assessment)		Access: Engage: Express:
Reflection		

Source: Personalize Learning, LLC.

Conversation Starters

- What did you discover that you are doing differently in this lesson?
- What did you learn from this process in designing this lesson?
- How did Access, Engage, and Express help you come up with instructional strategies for your learners?

Next Steps

The UDL Lesson Review and Lesson Design process involves thinking differently about how you select methods and materials based on who your learners are in the CLS. Some learners may need more intensive intervention, and a different level of support should be provided. At the end of your lesson, provide time for the learners to talk about their learning and how it may connect with prior learning. Providing learners this opportunity contributes to their growth in becoming self-directed learners.

Chapter 7 will expand on the lesson and design process you learned in this chapter by exploring deeper learning through project-based learning, inquiry, and assessment.

Build the Common Language

Add the common language to the list that you started from the previous chapters.

- Consider the common language and how it will be introduced to your learners as you present your lessons.
- What new language and ideas did you discover in the lesson design that you will use in your lessons?

Review: Keep a daily journal on your reflections and what you learned about your lessons and learners.

Learn: What instructional methods worked and did not work as you delivered your initial lessons and how did you adjust?

Apply: How will you apply these lesson processes in daily practice?

7

Delve Into Deeper Learning

How can I create an environment that encourages deeper learning?

This chapter is about going deeper into learning and how learners use voice and choice. When learners have agency, they are taking ideas and concepts deeper. The learning environment changes. The culture and climate in the classroom changes. Yet these changes do not happen right away. Students at the Center, studentsatthecenter.org, developed a grounded definition of learner-centered learning with these four key principles:

- Learning is personalized.
- Learning is **competency-based**.
- Learning takes place anytime, anywhere.
- Learners have agency and ownership over their learning.

These principles, guided by a rigorous set of goals, provide a strong foundation for the pursuit of deeper learning—the knowledge, skills, and dispositions necessary to prepare every learner for college, career, and civic life.

In this chapter, we will be integrating the concepts around personalized learner-centered environments and the elements of learner agency as we expand on the lesson activities in Chapter 6 to project-based learning activities. Figure 7.1 provides an illustration of the process of deeper learning through project-based learning.

Figure 7.1   Deeper Learning Process

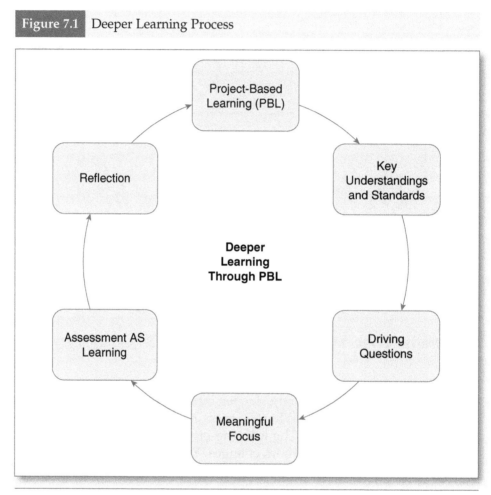

Source: Personalize Learning, LLC.

The takeaways will be strategies to encourage learners to

- understand how to encourage voice and choice in project-based learning (PBL);
- determine key understandings and standards;
- develop driving questions that encourage deeper learning;
- choose meaningful and relevant focus for PBL;
- assess as they learn by demonstrating evidence of learning; and
- reflect and notice learning during the process.

PROJECT-BASED LEARNING

Project-based learning (PBL) incorporates the elements of personalized, learner-centered environments. Developing projects where learners create the same product is different from PBL. Projects are about the product, whereas PBL is about the process.

> "*PBL provides learners with the opportunity to learn content at their own pace and with a great depth because the project is HOW they learn the content. Projects are often after the unit is completed and are an add on rather than a real learning experience.*" Linda Ullah, Personalize Learning Coach, PBL Consultant

The learning process is more personalized with PBL activities when learners are encouraged to ask questions, and then modify their ideas based on individual and collective responses to those questions. PBL projects serve as a strategy to allow learners to play, experiment, do meaningful tasks, and collaborate with peers and community members on local and global issues. Table 7.1 describes the differences between PBL and simply doing projects.

Table 7.1   PBL versus Projects

Project-Based Learning	Projects
Is based on a driving question generated by learners and teacher	Are designed and guided by teacher
Includes "Needs to Know" by learners	Are outlined with expectations by teacher
Encourages learners to make choices or come up with ideas throughout project	Do not provide many opportunities to make choices during project
Is timely, is complex, meets multiple standards, and is focused on the process with different products	Tend to be used multiple years creating same product for all learners and are done "like last year"
Can investigate real-world problems and provide solutions even if not implemented	Are not used to solve real-world problems
Is relevant to learners' lives and their future	Are not particularly relevant to learners
Uses tools appropriately for the task and purpose of the project	Are sometimes used to teach a tool for the project
Uses open questions from learners who determine outcome for process and product	Start with closed question from teacher who designs project with same goal for all learners

Source: Personalize Learning, LLC—adapted from Amy Mayer (2015), *The Difference Between Projects and Project-Based Learning.*

PBL involves rigorous and relevant standards-focused projects that engage learners in authentic learning activities, teach 21st-century skills, and demand demonstration of mastery. PBL essentially involves

- learners learning knowledge to tackle realistic problems as they would be solved in the real world;
- increased learner control over his or her learning;
- teachers serving as coaches and facilitators of inquiry and reflection; and
- learners (usually, but not always) working in pairs or groups.

PBL Planning Form

The PBL Planning Form (Table 7.2) adapted from the Buck Institute for Education (BIE.org) is available on the companion website. The teacher can introduce the form to the learners and then walk them through each of the sections. More information is detailed in Table 7.3 with methods the teacher can use to transform teaching and what to include for learning strategies to encourage voice and choice.

Table 7.2   7.2 PBL Planning Form

Title of Project:		Date:
Name(s):		Duration:
Standards		
Focus		
Roles		
Driving Question		
Content Areas		
Competencies or Skills		
Summary		
Entry Event		
Products		
Resources		
Assessment		
Rubric		
Reflection		

Source: Adapted from Buck Institute for Education (BIE). (n.d.)

PBL Methods and Strategies

Table 7.3 demonstrates how the teacher can introduce voice and choice to give learners more responsibility for their learning in PBL. Each section of the planning form (Table 7.2) is detailed with instructional methods for the teacher and suggested learning strategies for learners. Table 7.3 provides suggestions for teachers to use but does not include a complete list of methods and strategies.

KEY UNDERSTANDINGS AND LEARNING STANDARDS

So let's go back to the book, *Roll of Thunder, Hear My Cry* (Taylor, 1976) and the key understandings learners had when they read and discussed the book in class. This will help learners determine how they meet the standards and understand the message the book's author is trying to get across. This book takes on issues based on historical facts that are difficult to grasp today: lynchings, burnings, terror caused by nightmen, sharecropping, and other racist situations that were a reality in the South in the 1930s. All of this was woven into the economic problems of the Depression. This may be the first time learners are introduced to the concepts of buying things on credit along with paying mortgages and property taxes. This book is also about family and community, learners could relate to. This book opens their eyes to multiple topics to discuss as a whole class or in small groups. Consider doing the following activity around standards to help learners determine the focus or topic for their projects.

Table 7.3 PBL Instructional Methods and Learning Strategies

	Instructional Methods	Learning Strategies
Title	Teacher introduces planning form and explains why good titles can grab people's attention. Teacher provides examples for catchy titles, e.g., *How can Racism be Stopped?* *Lessons from the Great Depression*	Learners do research on catchy titles and brainstorm ideas so all group members have a voice in process. Learners write the title last after they fill out the PBL planning form. http://goinswriter.com/catchy-headlines/
Names	Teacher can guide the process for learners to choose the group to join based on the topic or question and asks each group to come up with a name for the group.	Learners choose the top three topics they would like to explore from Activity 7.1 relating to key understandings and standards. Learners select their groups, with no more than four to five in each group.
Standards	Teacher explains why they need to choose from the standards that they are expected to meet in the next six weeks. The teacher posts the standards and describes how learners can keep track of standards met.	Each group uses the process of the selection criteria for each standard group members chose in Activity 7.1. Each member of the group can be responsible for identifying one or two standards that the project will meet and track how they are meeting those standards.
Focus	Teacher guides the process for each group to choose a focus for its project based on the topic and group learners chose. If the topic is discrimination, then the focus could be either background of discrimination or how discrimination is currently affecting society.	Learners brainstorm ideas for the focus of their project around the topic or theme they chose for their group. Learners are encouraged to brainstorm as many ideas as possible without judgment. Then learners choose the top three ideas to discuss. Learners chronicle the process they took to choose the final focus for project.
Roles	Teacher gives examples of roles in the group: artist, researcher, writer, etc. Learners can take on multiple roles but each group needs to demonstrate how members plan to keep track of who is doing what by when.	Learners brainstorm ideas for different roles and who would be best for specific or multiple roles. Learners can determine how they plan to hold everyone accountable.
Duration	Teacher can define the timeline or leave this more open-ended depending on schedule. Teacher can create an optional checklist and timeline to keep on top of PBL.	Learners reflect on the process and how long it may take to complete specific tasks. Then they estimate duration for their projects. One member can keep track of the tasks and timeline using a checklist.
Driving Question	Teacher presents driving question activities with learners and shares qualities of questions around the topic.	Learners work collaboratively in their groups to create a driving question, identifying qualities in the driving question section and Activity 7.2.

	Teacher	Learner
Content Areas	Teacher explains that even though they are reading the book *Roll of Thunder, Hear My Cry*, they are learning about what it was like in the 1930s, especially for the Logan family. Several content areas other than English/Language Arts and social studies can be built into the PBL.	Learners reflect and discuss the types of activities they want to do for their projects. One group may research discrimination and create a skit to bring in the arts and role-play what happened to the Logans. Another group may design a business during that time and use math to design a spreadsheet.
Competencies or Skills	Teacher refers to and demonstrates learner competencies and skills learners may acquire with the PBL that could be the criteria for a rubric: critical thinking, collaboration, research, independent work, inquiry, voice, self-management, choice, etc.	Learners list and explain how they will meet competencies or skills based on the criteria in the rubric. They will provide evidence of learning by demonstrating that they have mastered that competency or developed the skill as part of their project.
Summary	Teacher provides an example of a summary under 100 words for the planning form and walks learners through strategies on summarizing and paraphrasing.	Learners include the issue, problem, or challenge in their project, the action they plan to take, the purpose for the project, and who will benefit from the project.
Entry Event	Teacher will provide examples of entry events, use the question, "How will you build engagement right from the beginning?," and invite Knows and Needs to Know. Teacher will ask groups to pitch ideas to class and show how to do constructive feedback.	Learners will brainstorm what they believe their audience will need to learn and what they will need to know for the project. They then will design or find a way to "hook" the audience, create a short summary, and pitch it to the class for constructive feedback.
Products	Teacher can demonstrate examples of products and provide guidance on how learners engage during the process and in creating the product.	Learners determine what will be the best medium to create a product that will demonstrate, persuade, or showcase their ideas for their project.
Resources	Teacher can share ideas and examples of resources available from inventory, people who have offered to help, materials, and community partners.	Learners will start and update the list of resources they will need for the product as they go through the process. Resources can include tools, materials, and people.
Assessment	Teacher can share multiple methods for assessment as learners demonstrate evidence of learning, e.g., collection of documents, images, and videos that is uploaded to the learner portfolio.	Learners determine what to collect for the group and individually as evidence of learning. They will check in often with each other to discuss and review evidence and review process.
Rubric	Teacher will design the rubric around the skills and competencies to meet in PBL and invite input from learners.	Learners provide input on the design of the rubric and include expectations for process and products.
Reflection	Teacher demonstrates strategies to reflect on process as they learn using journals, blogs, video, and audio notes.	Learners can individually journal and reflect on the process as they learn. They can opt to invite feedback from peers.

Source: Personalize Learning, LLC.

ACTIVITY 7.1
Articulating the Learning Standards

Brainstorm themes from the book, *Roll of Thunder, Hear my Cry* individually or in groups. This activity has two purposes: one to come up with a topic or theme for projects that learners are interested in researching, and the other is to develop the partnership level in learner voice as part of the process. We will use an example reading standard for learners for this activity.

(Example Reading Standard) Reading: Literature (*RL*) Standard 2: *Determine a theme or central idea of a text and how it is conveyed through particular details; provide a summary of the text distinct from personal opinions or judgments.*

Brainstorming (about 10 minutes)

1. Read the reading standard to the class and place a typed copy on the wall. Explain that learners will be responsible for choosing a theme or topic for their projects.

2. Have learners form groups of four and give them multiple Post-it notepads of different colors and one flip chart. Make sure groups are situated around the room.

> **Brainstorming Topics**
>
> Generate questions for themes or topics around the standard and book. When learners brainstorm using Post-it notes in a short amount of time, they bounce ideas off of each other.

1. Let learners know that they have only one minute to come up with as many themes they can, writing each theme or topic on a separate Post-it to place on their flip charts.

2. Have learners stop at one minute and discuss for two to three minutes with each other their topics considering these questions: *Do you see anything missing? Do you still have some ideas for more topics? Did you get any new ideas from reading other topics from the Post-its?*

3. Stop the discussions and tell them they have one more minute to add more topics. This is the fun part. Watch the learning happen. Then stop them exactly in one minute.

Selection Criteria (15 minutes)

1. Give each group color sticky dots (three different colors) so each person in the group has six dots: two of each color that they place on the Post-its:
   a. Most controversial (Green)
   b. I can relate to most (Yellow)
   c. Most interesting or exciting (Pink)

2. Have each group put all the green dots together, yellows together, and pinks together at the top of the flip chart.

3. Tell them to discuss the topics they selected and then prioritize the top three topics. Make sure everyone in the group has a voice in the process.

4. Each group will need to choose one topic and discuss some of the elements of the topic members would like to learn more about.

5. Have each group choose one person to share why the group chose this theme or topic from the book and why members are curious to learn more. The groups need to explain that they are keeping out any personal opinions and judgments. (Articulating RL Standard 2)

This brainstorming process can be adapted for any activity. After topics and themes have been selected, learners can stay with their group or change which group they would like to work with based on the topic.

Conversation Starters

After you try the brainstorming process with your learners, go to the Companion Website to answer these questions:

- What worked well when learners brainstormed together?
- Did all of the learners participate? How can you encourage learners who held back?
- Were any of the groups not able to summarize why they chose the topic and articulate the standard? What could you do differently to make sure they understand the process?

Know and Align Standards (Excerpt from article on Edutopia by Andrew Miller) www.edutopia.org/blog/6-strategies-truly-personalize-pbl-andrew-miller
There may come a time when learning will be so open that learners will be able to learn whatever they want. However, in this day and age, we are accountable to learning standards and outcomes. This doesn't mean that we can't be flexible in how we help learners reach these learning objectives. And personalized PBL can help us find that flexibility. As learners generate their questions, project ideas, and products for learning, teachers must align their work to standards and outcomes, which means that teachers need to know their standards deeply in order to serve as translators of learners' personalized projects to the standards. Teachers can create checklists of the standards, sub-standards, and outcomes to work through the "weeds" of hitting the standards through personalized projects, and they can use these checklists with learners to co-create project ideas and assessments. [Miller, 2015]

Andrew Miller serves on the National Faculty for the Buck Institute for Education and ASCD. He is author of Freedom to Fail *(2015).*

DRIVING QUESTIONS

How can we motivate learners and encourage deeper thinking in our classroom?
To understand the concept of deeper learning, consider John Dewey's theory of education, which begins with inquiry and the curiosity of the learner. Inquiry is about seeking knowledge, information, or truth through questioning.

> **Pause/Think/Reflect**
>
> How do you encourage your learners to take responsibility for building a solid understanding of the central concept of the story?

There are a variety of terms for a main question: essential question, driving question, big question, or focus question. To describe deeper learning in this book, we are using the term *driving question*.

Introducing the Inquiry Process

You can introduce and discuss the idea that good questions can drive deeper learning. Share that a driving question addresses an authentic, real-world challenge, issue, or dilemma that is intriguing or provocative enough for learners to discuss, inquire, and investigate a problem or specific topic.

Driving Questions

- Are open-ended and encourage more than only one answer
- Do not lead the learners but allow them to draw their own conclusions
- Are broad and challenging yet age appropriate
- Relate to learners' own lives, interests, or communities
- Are complex, but feasible to research in the time available, and require higher-level thinking skills such as evaluating and synthesizing information
- Provide multiple approaches to research and solving problems
- Go to the heart of the subject of study, focusing on central issues or controversies that are often debated by experts in the field and are a frequent topic of media attention
- Can lead to a presentable call to action, a plan, a campaign, a proposal, or recommendations for how to address the question

Multiple qualities will help learners focus their projects if the question is clear and has a focus that is challenging enough. In order to go deeper with a driving question, the qualities of driving questions are described next with examples and strategies in Table 7.4.

Open/Closed Questions

There are two types of questions: open or closed. Closed questions only have one right answer. Open questions allow for unlimited answers that encourage discussions and even more questions.

Objective of a Question

A question that encourages deeper learning allows learners to draw their own conclusions and ideas. Or, a question could be leading and written so learners only have one way to answer it.

Focus of Project

The focus of a driving question needs to be broad and challenging for the entire project not just for one part of the project. Sometimes the focus is too narrow to be a driving question but it could be a supporting question.

Research and Reflection

A driving question needs to be appropriate for the age of the learners. It has to be challenging enough so research and reflection is required for understanding.

Prior Knowledge

A driving question needs to be built on concepts learners already understand and be appropriate for the project.

Relates to Learners' Lives

This quality involves driving questions that are relevant and age appropriate for the learners. The question also has to take in consideration the skills learners need to have and concepts being taught in the project.

Multiple Approaches to Problem-Solving

The driving question needs to allow multiple methods and Universal Design for Learning (UDL) strategies for learners to address their strengths in researching and answering the question.

Strategies to Go Deeper With Questions

Now review how questions do or do not meet some of the qualities of a driving question (Table 7.4).

Table 7.4   Strategies with Questions

Quality	Question Does Not Meet Quality	Problem	Question Meets Quality
Open/Closed Questions	What is the weather like in India today?	Question has only one answer.	How has the climate in India affected the development of Indian culture?
Objective of a Question	Why is exercise good for you?	Question is leading. Does not allow learners to draw their own conclusions based on facts.	What are the best exercises for you and why?
Focus of Project	Project: Drug Education How does smoking marijuana affect your health?	Question is too narrow and needs to be broad and challenging enough to focus the entire project, not just one or two discussions.	Project: Drug Education How do drugs affect our health?
Research and Reflection	For fourth grade, How many fingers do you have?	Question is not age-appropriate and does not require research or reflection.	For fourth grade, How would life be different if you had no fingers?
Prior Knowledge	For sixth grade, What kind of specialized fighting techniques did the Scandinavians use?	Question is not age-appropriate and does not allow learners to build on something they already understand.	For sixth grade, How does the climate and terrain of a land affect the way we live?
Relates to Learners' Lives	What is a law?	Question does not relate basic skills and concepts to learners' lives.	How do laws affect how we live?
Multiple Approaches to Problem-Solving	How many billboards are in your neighborhood?	Does not allow for multiple ways to express the solution. Question needs to allow children with different strengths to learn.	What are the features of a good advertisement?

Source: Personalize Learning, LLC , adapted from http://www.jetspost.com/eportfolio/pbl/driving_questions .htm

Now let's expand on the sixth-grade lesson activity for *Roll of Thunder, Hear My Cry* by Mildred Taylor that we used in Chapter 6. Before the learners read the book, you can determine their prior knowledge of the time period and their understanding of the concepts in the story of an African American family in 1930s Mississippi with using the driving questions developed in Activity 7.2. You can share that this story is historical fiction and is a tale of the struggles that families such as the

Logans faced with racism and of the strength they found in family. It is also a story about how staying true to one's values can involve pride, but also involves sacrifice and risk.

ACTIVITY 7.2
Qualities of a Driving Question

Now it's your turn. Let's go back to the activity for the book, *Roll of Thunder, Hear My Cry*. See if you can do this first yourself.

1. Download Table 7.5 on the Companion Website.

2. Look at the quality in the questions listed below.

3. Fill in the problem with each question.

4. Then create new questions to put in right column that meet the qualities listed in the left column.

5. Share your questions with another teacher to see if they meet the quality.

Table 7.5 Driving Question Quality

Quality	Question Does Not Meet Quality	Problem	Question Meets Quality
Open/Closed	When did former slaves get the rights of full citizenship?		
Prior Knowledge	What was the Great Depression?		
Relate to Learner's Life	How did Cassie's family support each other?		
Focus of Project	What was sharecropping?		

Source: Personalize Learning, LLC.

In this activity, we dissected the questions about the qualities to come up with deeper questions that you can choose from for the driving question. Some questions to share with your learners after doing this activity:

- Which new question that meets the quality sounds like a driving question? Why?
- Did you come up with a better driving question? If so, share it.
- Consider using your own content to come up with questions for this activity.

Conversation Starters

Consider other teachers who take a chance to encourage learners to create driving questions. Use these questions to build the conversations with other educators who are reading this chapter:

- What worked well when learners designed the driving question?
- What concerns do you have about learners creating the driving question?
- What would you like to try next and do you have any questions from other teachers?

To understand why inquiry and questions encourage learners to express themselves and own their learning, we invited Starr Sackstein to share why it is important to put the power of questions in learners' hands.

Putting the Power of Questions in the Learner's Hands

By Starr Sackstein

Every child has the power to develop the journey that is her or his learning. Unfortunately, too often they are robbed of this opportunity by well-meaning teachers who have planned so perfectly so as to create the questions and answers to all of the lessons. What teachers need to understand is that by planning the specifics of the guiding questions, we take away a valuable chance to include learners in the process and add value and engagement to the experience.

Children are full of questions. We must teach them how to focus their questions and then how to find their own answers within the content areas we teach.

Imagine providing learners with some background material for a text or history and then asking them to explore it in a way that works for them. Then either in small groups at first and maybe later individually ask them to develop a line of questioning to explore for that content. It's time to start saying yes to learner questions instead of "we can't go over that now because it isn't on the test!"

In my own classes, I have found that learners develop a deep level of inquiry when we provide agency of some kind and freedom. For example, when reading *A Christmas Carol* by Charles Dickens, after learners did research about different historical topics directly related to the text, the learners networked with each other to develop questions about their interests. The conversations varied from charity in the nineteenth century to modern-day iterations of the same as well as whether Scrooge actually changed. Learners led the discussion. They used text and then debated each other.

If I had tried to plan this lesson the way I did earlier in my career, we probably would have missed out on a deeper level of learner inquiry that continued for several days. It's time to make this change happen. Where can you add opportunities for learner questioning into your lessons?

Here are some ideas to get you started:

1. Develop stepping-stones in the classroom. Depending on the age and level of the learners, consider starting with building questions in pieces after teaching parts of Bloom's Taxonomy. If learners understand what makes a "good" question, one that will be open instead of closed, they are more likely to ask a question that will yield more depth of understanding and improve their learning experiences.

2. Teach learners to dissect questions and reconstruct them as needed. Teach learners to approach questions differently to help them understand questions better. They can dissect and reconstruct questions the same way writing pieces will help them develop questions as a group and alone, digging deeper into diction choice and the subtly of word meaning.

www.personalizelearning
.com/2016/01/putting-power-
of-questions-in-learners.html

3. Empower learners with the control of the questions to put them in the driver's seat of their journeys and progress. Have them follow their interests to develop more questions as they go, unraveling the possibilities in their learning. This is a great chance for learners and teachers to learn together rather than just in a one-sided manner with the teacher in control of everything.

Starr Sackstein @MsSackstein, is a high school English and journalism teacher at World Journalism Preparatory School in Flushing, New York, where her learners run a multimedia news outlet at WJPSnews.com. Starr is the author of The Power of Questioning *(2016).*

MEANINGFUL AND RELEVANT FOCUS

When you design a project that encourages deeper learning, you will probably involve multiple standards around a theme that resonates with your learners. We invited Jackie Gerstein to share how you can make a project relevant and meaningful for your learners.

Learning Can Be Natural and Meaningful

By Jackie Gerstein, EdD, Faculty Online Teaching and Learning

The more you can apply what you're learning to your every day, the more it'll stick in your head. The reason is simple. When you're learning by doing, you're implementing everything that makes our memory work. When you're able to connect what you're learning with a real world task, that forms the bonds in your brain, and subsequently the skills you're learning will stick around.

Learners will find that they are meeting multiple standards since they will be researching, writing, and presenting. They may involve other subjects and standards depending on the tasks involved. Secondary learners can consult with other content teachers for ways to bring in standards from core content areas and electives. Jackie Gerstein illustrates in Figure 7.2 and explains how you can apply new learning in meaningful context.

Figure 7.2   Learning Facts Without a Context

Image Source: Jackie Gerstein, EdD

When I think about learning without a context, I get a visual image of all of these unconnected facts floating around in the learner's brain (Figure 7.2). Since they have nothing to connect to, they end up flying away. This is especially true for abstract concepts.

Learning facts and knowledge about a content area topic is an important prerequisite to understanding that topic and then developing expertise. The key to this understanding is providing a context for the facts. The context becomes the glue to increase the stickiness, the longevity of long-term memory of those facts. This is especially true for abstract concepts. These concepts need something concrete with which to attach.

Questions to Help Guide Learning

I believe it is each and every educator's responsibility to ensure that their teaching strategies match both best practices in education and the learning needs of their students. What follows are some general evaluation questions to begin the process of this congruence:

- Is failure viewed as normal and as a productive part of the learning process?
- Is learning spaced out over time rather than crammed into a short time period?
- Are distractions during learning normalized?
- Is the learning practiced often and in a variety of contexts?
- Is learning playful and fun? This is especially important when one gets "stuck" at an impasse.

Jackie Gerstein currently teaches master's-level online courses in educational technology for Boise State, American Intercontinental, and Western Governors universities. Jackie actively blogs at https://usergenerated education.wordpress.com/ and tweets at https:// twitter.com/jackiegerstein

www.personalizelearning
.com/2015/04/learning-can-
and-should-be-natural-and.html

Knows and Needs to Know

When each group reviews the resources and strategies the group members will need to develop their projects around the focus, they may find they need some resources or other people to support their projects—for example, background actors or musicians. Group members also may find that they need to acquire certain skills because they might not know how to use certain apps or tools or even how to work effectively in a group. The teacher can use something as simple as a flip chart, marking pens, Post-it notes, or an online interactive tool such as Padlet and define Knows and Needs to Know as they relate to the content, process, and project (Table 7.6). For the Knows, invite learners to share what they know and can teach others. Ask each learner to identify any Needs to Know such as skills or resources to place on the chart or Padlet with the name of the group and name of individual member if group members need help with a specific skill or resource.

Table 7.6 Knows and Needs to Know Example

Process	Knows	Needs to Know
Content	• Teaching Tolerance resources—Group 1 • Watched Grapes of Wrath—Group 2	• Research on the Great Depression—Group 3 • More information on racism in the 1930s and today—Group 1
Process	• Organizing groups—Group 3 • Acting and scriptwriting—Group 2 (Mary)	• Tracking progress—Group 2 (John) • Another iPad for filming—Group 1 • 2 people as actors—Group 2
Product	• Film with iPad—Group 1 • Presentation skills—Group 3 (Michael)	• Summarize Pitch—Group 2 • Upload videos—Group 1

Source: Personalize Learning, LLC.

The teacher can check in with each group to see if any group or specific learner may not have had particular needs from individuals in the group addressed. Learners can refer to the chart for resources or other learners that can help them with their projects. Each group is building skills around teamwork and collaboration as they pull together to make the choices they need for the project. As learners are working in groups, the teacher can sit with each group to answer questions or meet one-on-one with a learner who needs additional support or help with a skill or question. Not all learners are confident that they have the skills and strategies to participate effectively as part of a group project. This is the time each learner's voice can be validated because of the time the teacher can put aside for any learner who is struggling with the process. Refer to Figure 7.3 to see where the learners are in the process of building their skills and strategies while challenging themselves and building confidence around the project.

Figure 7.3 PBL Challenge and Skills

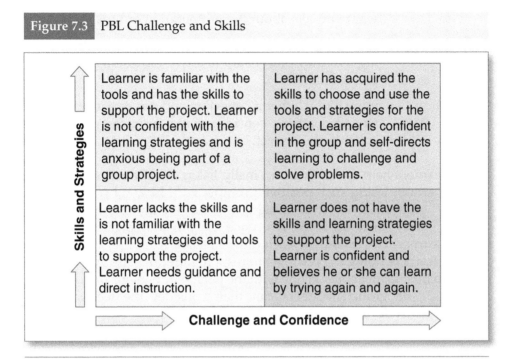

Skills and Strategies ↑	Learner is familiar with the tools and has the skills to support the project. Learner is not confident with the learning strategies and is anxious being part of a group project.	Learner has acquired the skills to choose and use the tools and strategies for the project. Learner is confident in the group and self-directs learning to challenge and solve problems.
↑	Learner lacks the skills and is not familiar with the learning strategies and tools to support the project. Learner needs guidance and direct instruction.	Learner does not have the skills and learning strategies to support the project. Learner is confident and believes he or she can learn by trying again and again.

Challenge and Confidence

Source: Personalize Learning, LLC.

This is where you can bring back their Learner Profiles (LPs) to encourage learners to address their strengths and interests during the project. As we wrote in earlier chapters, it is all about the conversations and the relationship between the learner and teacher. If you can find time to notice if a learner is struggling, then take more time to go deeper to find out if lack of confidence and skills might keep the learner from participating effectively in her or his group and in the learning process.

The Pitch and Feedback

After each group creates the entry event or "hook" for the group's project, group members can pitch the project to the class. The "hook" is a short motivating presentation under five minutes that could include the entry event as a slide show, video, poem, rap, song, dance, or short play. After group members give the presentation, they can share why they chose this topic, the process they took, and why they chose the medium they did for the entry event and pitch.

This process helps the group members focus and encourages others to listen and respond with constructive feedback. As they watch and listen to each group, all learners in the class use Post-it notes or apps to capture anything that stands out using these three prompts to share with the presenting group:

I like . . .	what you like about the presentation or idea.
I wish . . .	something you wish did or didn't happen such as wishing that they didn't stop to answer questions during the presentation.
I wonder . . .	more like a "what if" question and can be something like having learners consider some resources that might enhance the project.

When learners help each other and really listen, it validates each learner and the group. Using such positive prompts as "I like," "I wish," and "I wonder" guides learners in framing how they give and receive feedback to each other (Hinckley, 2015). Everyone likes to hear positive feedback first so learners can encourage each other to share what they like.

The learners doing the pitch get to respond after this feedback is given or set up time to meet one on one with the person or persons providing the feedback. The group members can then consider the feedback they received when developing their project.

 Conversation Starters

- How can you address the learners' confidence in learning?
- How can the pitch help learners build confidence?
- How did learners react to being in groups, pitching their ideas, and providing constructive feedback to each other?

ASSESSMENT AS LEARNING

We believe assessment and reflection needs to be an ongoing process. In our book, *Make Learning Personal* (2015), we describe the differences between **assessment OF, FOR,** and **AS learning.** The goal is for assessment to be used AS learning, so that learners monitor their progress and reflect on their learning during the entire learning process.

Assessment AS learning is based in research about how learning happens and is characterized by learners reflecting on their own learning and making adjustments so that they achieve deeper understanding. The teacher's role in promoting the development of agency and independent learners through assessment as learning is to

- model and teach the skills of self-assessment;
- guide learners in setting goals and monitoring their progress toward them;
- provide exemplars and models of good practice and quality work that reflect curriculum outcomes;

- work with learners to develop clear criteria of good practice;
- guide learners in developing internal feedback or self-monitoring mechanisms to validate and question their own thinking and to become comfortable with the ambiguity and uncertainty that is inevitable in learning anything new;
- provide regular and challenging opportunities to practice, so that learners can become confident, competent self-assessors;
- monitor learners' metacognitive processes as well as their learning and provide descriptive feedback; and
- create an environment where it is safe for learners to take chances and where support is readily available.

Reporting in assessment AS learning is the responsibility of learners, who can learn to articulate and defend the nature and quality of their learning. When learners reflect on their own learning and communicate it to others, they are intensifying their understanding about a topic, their own learning strengths, and the areas in which they need to develop further.

PBL Rubric Design

We provide the PBL Rubric Design to aid learners in assessing their own learning. Learners are more involved in assessing how they learn as they are learning. The PBL Rubric provides a process for learners to address all the elements that are to be included in their projects.

A rubric includes descriptors for specific skills or levels of performance. Rubrics are supposed to be descriptive, and not evaluative. Rubrics are as good or bad as the criteria selected and descriptions under each level. General rubrics generalize across the levels and can be used with different tasks instead of task specific descriptions. General rubrics focus on the knowledge and skills learners are learning rather than on the particular tasks they are doing.

Learners can use the rubric to address learning goals, competencies, and skills that can be an integral part of the rubric creation process. Teachers can work with learners (especially if this is new to the learners or if they are young learners) to co-create the rubrics. As learners become more experienced, they can create their own rubrics with teacher guidance and with the teacher's final approval of the rubric, or this could be another pitch to the class with the class refining and selecting the rubrics that will be used. Rubrics need to be clearly linked to what is to be learned (including 21st-century skills, Habits of Mind, standards, "I Can" statements, etc.). The teacher can guide the process around competencies and skill development along with learning targets that are addressed in the project. Table 7.7 provides an example rubric with two criteria and descriptions for project process and design.

> **Pause/Think/Reflect**
>
> Good rubrics focus on "learning" and not what a teacher intends to teach.

Table 7.7 Example Criteria and Descriptions for Rubric for Project Process and Design

Criteria	Lacks Features	Needs Further Development	Masters Skills and Knowledge
Inquiry	• Has a single or simple answer • Does not relate to project or focus of problem • Does not engage learners in process	• Level of challenge is inappropriate for learners • Relates to project but does not capture problem or topic • Includes some but not all features of driving question	• Focuses on problem and is appropriate challenge level • Open-ended encouraging multiple answers • Aligned with learning goals and targets
Authenticity	• Lacks real-world tasks • Does not make a real impact on the world • Does not address learners' interests	• May have limited features or feel contrived • Has some authentic features	• Includes real-world tasks • Makes a difference or impact • Addresses learners' interests or concerns

Source: Personalize Learning, LLC.

There are multiple examples of rubrics related to design, process, key skills and understandings, reflections, products, and more. Sample forms and links to resources including rubric generators can be found on the Companion Website.

 Conversation Starters

- How will you use what you've learned by doing this project as you approach your next project?
- What went well?
- What might you do differently?
- How did this process work for you?

After we started writing about PBL, we interviewed Paula Ford, a kindergarten teacher in a Title I school in California about her project with her young learners. She shared that there are over 29 languages spoken at her school, which is in year 2 of transitioning to a science, technology, engineering, and mathematics (STEM) project-based learning school. One reason we want to share her story is for you to know that kindergarteners are up to tackling challenges, can use inquiry, and can be creative and innovative.

Project-Based Learning Gives Kindergarteners Agency

By Paula Ford, Kindergarten Teacher, Manuel De Vargas
Elementary School in San Jose, California

My kindergarteners decided they wanted to collect books to send to kids at the Cheery Education Center in Kenya in Africa. Their plan was to decorate boxes, put them by classrooms, and have the whole school bring in donations. The kids decided the focus instead of me. They decided to make a video explaining our project-based learning (PBL) activity to ask for help from all the classes in the school.

We found out it cost over $65.00 to ship a medium-sized box to the Cheery Education Center in Africa. I brought the box into class and then we saw that it only held eight books. So, we went back to our "what do we know" information and realized that it costs $50 for two children to attend school with meals for a month in Africa. That seemed like a more realistic project compared to sending eight books for $65.00. The kids decided to collect coins and came up with the collection jars called "Change for Change."

The kids chose the groups to work on speeches for their video presentations. Each group had a different subtopic on our Africa PBL. Then we worked with our fourth-grade buddies to practice fluency, voice projection, eye contact, etc. We filmed it in front of the Chroma Key Green Screen with the big buddies watching the filming.

Some of the kinder kids made African-inspired crafts to sell at a "pop-up store" on campus to donate the money to the African school. They figured out pricing and ran the store during recess, at lunch, and after school. Another group of kinders wanted to make a webpage with help from the class in the designing process. They put up some artwork and writings of what they have learned. In PE, the kids learned African dances. I have been teaching them all African rhythms with the rhythm sticks (great for learning syllables). In science, they learned about what people need to survive focusing on our PBL in Africa. Our collection jars, "Change for Change," are now in every class-room. My kids have made four videos for our video announcements about Africa.

Paula Ford, @prford5, taught kindergarten, first grade, and third grade and has been a resource teacher for grades transitional kindergarten through fifth grade. The majority of her career has been teaching low-socioeconomic English language learners. Currently, she teaches kindergarten at Manuel De Vargas Elementary School.

Read the full post at http://www.personalizelearning.com/2016/03/project-based-learning-gives.html

REFLECTION MAKES LEARNING VISIBLE

Starting with the learner is all about focusing on learning and noticing how we learn. This is about making learning visible. For too long, the focus has been on instruction and test scores. It was all about teaching subjects, and testing. In his book *Learning: A Sense-Maker's Guide* (2003), Chris Watkins provides four teaching practices that can help learners and teachers make sense of their learning, as shown in Figure 7.4.

Figure 7.4   Cycle of Learning

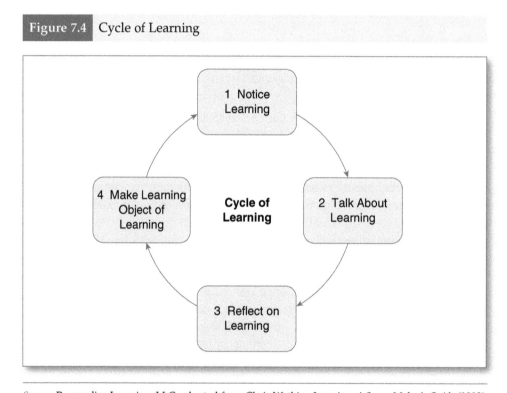

Source: Personalize Learning, LLC, adapted from Chris Watkins *Learning: A Sense-Maker's Guide (2003)*.

Watkins is a researcher and leading authority on learner-centered environments in the United Kingdom, and we highly recommend that you read and follow his work at http://chriswatkins.net. He has helped us clarify why we need to transform learning and emphasized the importance to focus on learning not teaching.

When you see learners noticing and reflecting on their learning during their learning, that is the "Wow" of learning. This is called the *Cycle of Learning*. These are the higher-order thinking skills we want our children to adopt: learning about learning (meta-learning) and thinking about learning (metacognition). This makes learning visible. This is what shakes up the classroom dynamics because when the teacher is lecturing, learners are supposed to be listening. Are they? When you shake up the learning so that it is visible and learners are talking about their learning, the classroom environment is different. We adapted Watkins' model with specific strategies the teacher can ask or have the learners ask themselves or each other. The questions or directions as prompts are listed under each of the four teaching practices.

1. **Notice learning**

   Ask learners to step back and notice what happened when they were learning with these questions:

   a. What did we do to make learning happen?
   b. What were the effects?
   c. How did it feel?
   d. What helped you learn?
   e. How did you persist to make learning happen?
   f. What might you do with the learning that just happened?

2. **Have conversations about learning**

   Ask learners to pair or work in groups of three or four and discuss what they noticed in their learning. Use these questions as prompts:

   a. Why we did _____ yesterday?
   b. Did we find out anything new?
   c. How can we find out more?

3. **Reflect on your learning**

   Reflection helps learners notice learning because they think about it when they write. Use these statements as prompts for your learners:

   a. Keep a personal journal or blog.
   b. Write about your learning as it happens.
   c. Write any new ideas that come to you about your learning that you never knew before.

4. **Make learning an object of learning**

   Learners can learn about learning while they are learning about something else.

   a. When learners are reading or doing research, have them reflect on what and how they learned.
   b. Ask them how they handled their feelings as they were learning.
   c. Encourage them to reflect how they engaged with others as they learned.

After we read Watkins' *Learning: A Sense-Maker's Guide*, it was clear to us that if you make learning an object of learning, it makes learning visible. The four classroom practices described earlier build on each other and lead to a key ingredient in effective learning that develops learners with agency.

> **Consider This!**
>
> If you really want learning to go deeper in daily practice, it is more than engaging learners' voices on learning. It is about giving them an opportunity to understand their learning. Using the four classroom practices will help learners make meaningful and relevant connections to their learning.

When we talked to teachers who went deeper, took risks, and personalized learning, many told us they would never go back to traditional teaching.

Reflection Is for Teachers Too!

Pernille Ripp, a seventh-grade teacher in Oregon, Wisconsin, helps learners discover their superpowers. Pernille wrote her book, *Passionate Learners* (2015), because she believed there had to be a better way of preparing children for their future. She shares her personal story and reflection about transforming the culture of learning in her classroom.

Beginning of the End of Supreme Bringer of Knowledge

By Pernille Ripp, Seventh-Grade Teacher,
Oregon School District, Wisconsin

Embracing Personalized Learning

Almost 6 years into my transformation as a teacher who embraces personalizing learning as much as possible, I would never go back to the way it was before. The drastic changes I made back then have now become insignificant in the best possible way; they are no longer terrifying, nor are they dramatic, but instead they are woven into the very tapestry of the way we function as a learning community. It is a given that there is choice in our classroom, that there is an ongoing conversation regarding the way they are learning, what they are learning, and how they will be assessed. That learners may use the environment in the way that makes the most sense for them and use each other as they try to engage with materials.

The changes we have now are so integrated that I sometimes fail to see the marvel in them; we just work as a learning community, yet to others, to try to replicate this type of learning community may seem just as terrifying as it did to me so many years ago. Yet the beauty of personalized learning is that even the smallest changes can make the biggest difference. That you should keep the end goal in mind but always keep your eye on the steps right in front of you. Because if you do not, then personalized learning can seem overwhelming at best, impossible at worst. So how does one start toward a more personalized learning environment even within our sometimes regimented public school system?

Listening to My Learners

We start by asking our learners which needs they have that are not being met. We then listen to their answers and try to develop pathways that may include their requested modifications. One thing my learners asked for repeatedly was simply choice in what they created, something that is so easy to give and yet often overlooked. However, when it comes to creation, the power of the times that we live in is remarkable; learners have access to so many tools that can support them in their explorations. No longer do our choices have to be between PowerPoint and a poster, but instead can be left open to the tools that learners often access outside of school, outside of their supposed learning.

Simply by asking my learners more questions has expanded my knowledge of what is possible exponentially. Asking learners questions can be done in many ways. Now that I teach seventh grade, I do not have as much face-to-face time with my learners as I long for. Often our conversations happen through surveys or quick Google forms as I check in with them on their learning. Large group meetings, informal check-ins, small groups, and one-to-one teaching all have a part in it as well as we grow comfortable with each other and start to trust the notion that we are learning together. And for that learning to be powerful, my voice cannot be the loudest.

Realizing Education Is for Our Kids and Their Future

Six years ago, I set out on a journey that would challenge my belief that education was an institution that could not be changed, but instead had to be blindly followed no matter the collateral damage in its wake. I now know that the day I started asking my learners what changes they needed to become more engaged learners was the day that I made a difference in the way education can be used. Yet this change is fundamentally not about me. It is about the learners I teach, and it is for them that we must embrace a more meaningful way of educating. Call it personalizing learning or some other title, but in the end, we must make the very education that we are stewards of become about the kids that we teach again. (Ripp, 2016)

http://www .personalizelearning. com/2016/01/ my-transformation-as- teacher.html

Teachers also told us that the culture in the classroom changed so their colleagues were curious and wanted to learn more about personalized learning. During this process, teachers collaborated to design meaningful activities and PBL. Parents mentioned that their children were more excited about school especially when what they were studying was relevant to them. Chapter 8 introduces the elements of Learner Agency across the new version of the Stages of Personalized Learning Environments.

Build the Common Language

Add the common language to the list that you started from the previous chapters.

1. What common language did you discover in this chapter that is key to delve into deeper learning?

2. How does that common language of deeper learning connect with the common language from Chapter 6 on lesson design?

3. Update your common language after what you learned about transforming teaching and learning on the Padlet in the Companion Website.

Review: Write a reflection on the inquiry and how it worked with your learners and your own perception of how the process went.

Learn: Listen to your learners during the project-based learning activities and see what is working and what is not working.

Apply: Chronicle the learning happening, interview your learners as they learn, discuss with colleagues, and share successes with the school community.

8

Learner Agency Across the Stages

We originally created the Stages of Personalized Learning Environments (PLE) after teachers reviewed the Personalization vs. Differentiation vs. Individualization (PDI) chart. After some teachers reviewed the PDI chart, they asked us questions about their concerns about turning the learning over to the learners too fast. They also had questions about what to do with resistant learners or if they didn't have the ability to change the way they teach. We wanted to show teachers that they can go slower and dip their toes into personalized learning with Stage One. We wanted to show that moving to learner-centered environments does take time and a process.

STAGES OF PERSONALIZED LEARNING ENVIRONMENTS (PLE) AND LEARNER AGENCY

Let's take a closer look at the Stages of PLE version 5 (Figure 8.1) and how we can create learners with agency by helping them develop the skills at each stage with the elements of learner agency that we discussed in Chapter 3. Those who have read our book, *Make Learning Personal* (Bray & McClaskey, 2015), may be familiar with the Stages of PLE version 3, which we've now updated to version 5. If you have not read our previous book, version 5 of the Stages of PLE will be described in more detail in this section, plus there is a copy of the new version of the Stages of PLE on the inside of the back cover.

Figure 8.1 Stages of Personalized Learning Environments (PLE) v5

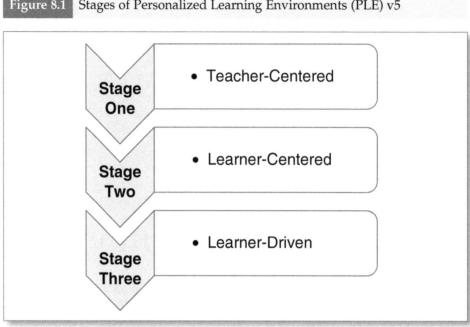

Source: Personalize Learning, LLC.

Stage One PLE (Teacher-Centered) Is Where the Teacher

- understands how each learner learns based on the Learner Profile (LP) and data;
- makes instructional decisions on methods and materials based on four diverse learners' LPs to create a Class Learning Snapshot (CLS);
- refers to the CLS to redesign the learning environment by changing the physical layout of classroom;
- universally designs instruction and materials to engage and guide learners in establishing learning goals in Personal Learning Plans (PLPs);
- revises lessons and projects that encourage learner voice and choice;
- designs activities to include tools and strategies that effectively instruct and engage all learners in the classroom;
- is introduced to **competency-based** learning—learning may still be part of a standards-driven, time-based grade-level system;
- (or counselor) suggests after-school and extracurricular activities to learners based on learning goals in PLPs; and
- uses existing or designs formative and summative assessment strategies and leads learner conferences with parents.

Now with the elements, we incorporated what that can mean for learners moving to agency starting in a **Stage One PLE** that is teacher-centered (Table 8.1).

Table 8.1   Elements of Learner Agency in Stage One PLE

Elements	In a Stage One PLE, the Learner
Voice	Establishes learning goals with the teacher based on strengths and challenges in the LP and provides feedback on the PLP
Choice	Chooses the learning environment for individual and group work and has a choice of learning activities, resources, and tools
Engagement	Builds relationships with teacher and peers and investigates topics with more choices in how he or she engages with content
Motivation	Seeks approval from the teacher and peers and is given opportunities to develop strategies that motivate the learner to meet learning goals in PLP
Ownership	Works with teacher on learning goals in PLP to develop and gain independent learning skills to support strengths and challenges in LP
Purpose	Identifies purpose for learning so the learner realizes who he or she is as a learner based on the LP and goals in PLP
Self-Efficacy	Is motivated by the choices he or she makes and is persistent in meeting learning goals in PLP

Source: Personalize Learning, LLC.

Stage Two PLE (Learner-Centered) Is Where the Learner

- with teacher guidance updates his or her LP by recognizing how learning changes;
- identifies learning strategies and skills with teacher to create actions steps for learning goals in the learner's PLP;
- co-designs the learning environment with multiple learning zones with teacher;
- with the teacher decides how he or she will best access information, engage with content, and express what the learner knows based on learning goals in PLP;
- and teacher are transforming lessons and projects together to include learner voice and choice;
- with teacher, acquires skills to choose and use the appropriate tools and strategies to access information, engage with content, and express what the learner knows and understands;
- demonstrates mastery of learning standards that may or may not be in a grade-level system transitioning to or are already in a competency-based system;
- and teacher work together to determine Extended Learning Opportunities (ELOs) based on college, career, personal, and citizenship goals in PLP; and
- contributes to the design of peer and self-assessment strategies and reflects on learning—The learner leads conferences with parents, teachers, and peers.

Let's look at what that means for learners moving to agency in a **Stage Two PLE** that is learner-centered (Table 8.2).

Table 8.2	Elements of Learner Agency in Stage Two PLE

Elements	In a Stage Two PLE, the Learner
Voice	Articulates action steps to meet learning goals in PLP and contributes to design of lessons, projects, and assessments
Choice	Chooses topics based on interests or questions and identifies ideas for designing activities, tasks, and roles for projects
Engagement	Explores interests, talents, and aspirations, connects with others with same interests, and enjoys learning from and teaching others
Motivation	Desires to succeed, persevere, and demonstrate mastery with evidence of learning in meeting goals in PLP
Ownership	Develops skills to work independently and creates PLP around college, career, citizenship, and personal goals
Purpose	Realizes opportunities that fulfill passions and interests, takes action about what matters for her or his growth, and is excited to try new things
Self-Efficacy	Focuses on task at hand and believes in his or her ability to develop skills to support learning

Source: Personalize Learning, LLC.

Stage Three PLE (Learner-Driven) Is Where the Learner

- monitors and adjusts his or her LP with the teacher as partner in learning;
- is an expert learner with agency who applies innovative strategies and skills to redesign and achieve learning goals in PLP;
- expands the learning environment in and outside school to include local and global community;
- self-directs how, when, and where he or she monitors, adjusts, and achieves learning goals in the PLP;
- designs challenging learning experiences based on the learner's interests, aspirations, passions, and talents;
- independently applies tools and strategies so he or she can explore deeper and more challenging experiences that extend learning and thinking;
- learns at he or she own pace and demonstrates mastery with evidence of learning in a competency-based system;

- self-selects ELOs based on college, career, personal, and citizen-ship goals as well as his or her interests, aspirations, passions, and purpose; and
- designs assessment and showcases evidence of learning through exhibitions that involve parents, peers, teachers, and community.

Let's look at what that means for learners moving to agency in a **Stage Three PLE** where learners own and drive learning (Table 8.3).

Table 8.3	Elements of Learner Agency in Stage Three PLE
Elements	**In a Stage Three PLE, the learner**
Voice	Identifies problems, generates solutions, guides group as a leader of change, and accepts responsibility for outcomes
Choice	Self-directs learning based on challenges, problems, or passions and chooses strategies, people, and resources to develop plan for action
Engagement	Is intrinsically motivated to pursue passions and purpose and is in control of and responsible for learning
Motivation	Is involved in learning for the love of learning and derives satisfaction from understanding, learning a skill, attaining knowledge, or creating something
Ownership	Self-monitors progress to adjust PLP as he or she meets goals and pursues interests and passions in innovative ways
Purpose	Desires a sense of purpose in the world where he or she chooses a problem or challenge to tackle looking beyond self-interests for a meaningful life
Self-Efficacy	Develops resilience for rigorous learning where he or she embraces challenges, takes risks, and views failure as a learning opportunity

Source: Personalize Learning, LLC.

CROSSWALK OF LEARNER AGENCY ACROSS THE STAGES OF PLE

We designed a crosswalk you can use to understand what it means for learners' voice, choice, and other elements of learner agency across the Stages of PLE (Table 8.4). This chart is available on the inside of the front cover and the Companion Website for teachers to review and determine which Stage of PLE they are in for each element and to share with their learners or colleagues.

Table 8.4   Crosswalk of Learner Agency Across the Stages

The Learner	Stage One Teacher-Centered	Stage Two Learner-Centered	Stage Three Learner-Driven
Voice	Establishes learning goals with the teacher based on strengths and challenges in the LP and provides feedback on the PLP.	Articulates action steps to meet learning goals in PLP and contributes to design of lessons, projects, and assessments.	Identifies problems, generates solutions, guides group as leader of change, and accepts responsibility for outcomes.
Choice	Chooses the environment for individual or group work and has a choice of learning activities, resources, and tools.	Chooses topics based on interests or questions and identifies ideas for designing activities, tasks, and roles for projects.	Self-directs learning based on challenges, problems, or passions and chooses strategies, people, and resources to develop plan for action.
Engagement	Builds relationships with teacher and peers and investigates topics with more choices in how he or she engages with content.	Explores interests, talents, and aspirations, connects with others with same interests, and enjoys learning from and teaching others.	Is intrinsically motivated to pursue passions and purpose and is in control of and responsible for learning.
Motivation	Seeks approval from teacher and peers and is given opportunities to develop strategies that motivate the learner to meet learning goals in PLP.	Desires to succeed, persevere, and demonstrate mastery with evidence of learning in meeting learning goals in PLP.	Is involved in learning for the love of learning and derives satisfaction from understanding, learning a skill, attaining knowledge, or creating something.
Ownership	Works with teacher on learning goals in PLP to develop and gain independent learning skills to support strengths and challenges in LP.	Develops skills to work independently and creates PLP around college, career, citizenship, and personal goals.	Self-monitors progress to adjust PLP as he or she meets goals and pursues interests and passions in innovative ways.
Purpose	Identifies purpose for learning so the learner realizes who he or she is as a learner based on the LP and goals in PLP.	Realizes opportunities that fulfill passions and interests, takes action about what matters for his or her growth, and is excited to try new things.	Desires a sense of purpose in the world where he or she chooses a problem or challenge to tackle looking beyond self-interests for a meaningful life.
Self-Efficacy	Is motivated by the choices he or she makes and is persistent in meeting learning goals in PLP.	Focuses on task at hand and believes in his or her ability to develop skills to support learning.	Develops resilience for rigorous learning where he or she embraces challenges, takes risks, and views failure as a learning opportunity.

Source: Personalize Learning, LLC.

ACTIVITY 8.1
Expanding the Crosswalk

How will teachers and administrators visualize the elements in each of the Stages of PLE? Use the previous crosswalk as a model for expanding with examples and models.

1. Download the Crosswalk Template on the Companion Website.

2. Create a Google Doc using the Crosswalk Template and invite teachers and leaders to provide links to examples and models that can be shared with your school or district.

Conversation Starters

- Compare the Stages of PLE v5 chart that is on the inside back cover with the crosswalk on the previous page and on the inside front cover.
- After reviewing the crosswalk of learner agency, consider what each stage means for your learners, you, and your role as a teacher, administrator, or parent.
- Share what stage your class or school is in and provide one or two specific examples using the elements of learner agency.

The crosswalk can help you identify where you are in the Stages of PLE with the elements of learner agency. We suggest referring to the crosswalk that is on the inside front cover of this book. As you start implementing some of the activities from this book and changing teaching practice, the culture changes. Chapter 9 is all about how to build a culture of learning as you go on your journey to personalize learning.

Build the Common Language

Add the common language to the list that you started from the previous chapters.

- What new language did you learn from reviewing the crosswalk of the elements of learner agency across the Stages of PLE and how does it connect with Chapter 3 on learner agency and the continuums?
- How could you use the common language in this chapter as you revisit your vision and shared beliefs?
- Update your common language on the Padlet on the Companion Website from the Stages of PLE and the elements of learner agency.

Review: What Stage of PLE is your class in? Where are your learners with each of the elements of learner agency?

Learn: How can you encourage learners to move through the Stages of PLE with the elements of learner agency?

Apply: How will you collect evidence of learning from learners to demonstrate mastery for each of the elements of learner agency?

9

Create a Culture of Learning

How do you build a positive culture based on trust and respect?

When you walk into a school, you can get a feel for the culture just by listening and seeing what is happening in the halls, classrooms, and faculty room. You can even invite teachers and learners to share what they think about school and how it helps them learn. What schools rarely do is discuss how important relationships are for learners and teachers. It does take a village to raise a child, just as Virgel Hammonds wrote in Chapter 1. The idea of school is changing and becoming more of a community for learners of all ages.

The takeaways for this chapter include how to

- build a **school culture** that cares about everyone in the community;
- understand the relationships between personal needs and school practice;
- design a learning environment that invites voice, choice, and engagement;
- do team building activities for the first few weeks of school;
- connect the dots of current practice to a Culture of Learning; and
- create a rationale for personalizing learning.

NURTURE A POSITIVE SCHOOL CULTURE

School leaders can nurture a positive culture that cares about everyone in the community. Kouzes and Posner (2008) have identified five practices of highly effective leaders that apply to culture in school settings:

1. **Model the way:** School leaders set an example for others to follow by establishing principles concerning the way teachers and learners need to be treated and how goals are to be met.

2. **Inspire a shared vision:** School leaders believe that they can make a difference and breathe life into their visions so all stakeholders see exciting possibilities for the future.

3. **Challenge the process:** School leaders search for opportunities to change the status quo and seek innovative ways to improve teaching and learning.

4. **Enable others to act:** School leaders foster collaboration in an environment based on trust and respect, making each person feel capable and powerful.

5. **Encourage the heart:** School leaders recognize contributions of individuals and celebrate accomplishments that make people feel like heroes.

> *"We learned that the birth of a vision requires the support of all stakeholders and the passion to make a difference for our learners."*
> Dr. Michelle Schmitz and Susan Maynor, EPiC Elementary

Building a positive culture with teachers, learners, and all stakeholders in the school community is all about encouraging the heart and building the relationships that matter. Relationships are a key component of every school community.

Relationships Between
Personal Needs Versus School Practices

School is all about relationships between teachers and learners and how the school provides flexible options for learning. Learners need to feel they are recognized, confirmed, and accepted as valuable parts of the community. When learners have a voice in their learning, the teacher and learner can work together as partners in learning.

The chart (Figure 9.1) was created by Brown University from research using observations of learners in typical high schools. The researchers identified specific criteria for learners' personal needs based on developmental needs, talents, and aspirations, which are on the left of the graphic. Researchers determined the need for flexible options for engaged learning in school practices, shown on the right of the graphic.

> "Teaching is some of kind of connection between people, not rules on a piece of paper."
> John Taylor Gatto

Figure 9.1 Personal Learning and Relationships

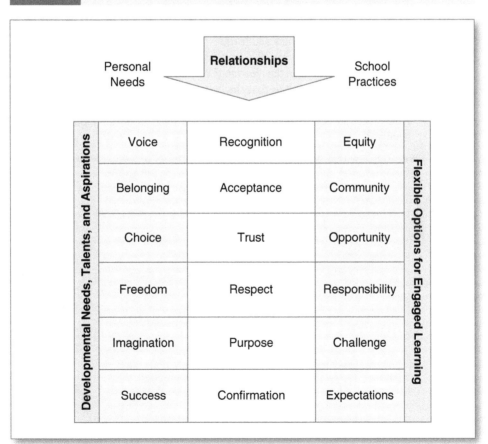

Source: Personalize Learning, LLC. Adapted from Clarke & Frazer (2003).

ACTIVITY 9.1
Build Relationships

This is a pair/share or small group activity. You can use the option to do this individually.

1. Download and read the research report "Making Learning Personal" from John H. Clarke and Edora Frazer (2003), available on the Companion Website.

2. Download the Table 9.1 Build Relationships document from the Companion Website to write your responses or to upload to a Google Doc to collaborate on your responses.

3. Choose one of the rows in Figure 9.1 to explore; for example, voice + equity = recognition.

4. Reflect on your own experience with the personal need and school practice you chose.

5. Discuss how and why the personal need and school practice you choose can affect relationships. Use these questions as prompts:
    a. What does it mean to encourage voice? How do you build an environment that encourages equity?
    b. Why is it important for learners to feel they belong and are accepted? How do you encourage learners to be active participants in the community?
    c. How do you give learners opportunities to choose how they learn? Why is trust necessary between teachers and learners?
    d. How much freedom can you give learners? How much responsibility can you give your learners so they drive their learning? Why does respect matter for relationships?
    e. How do you set up activities that challenge your learners? Where can you bring in imagination? How can learners discover their purpose?
    f. What does "success" mean? Why do learners need to develop expectations for learning?

Table 9.1	Build Relationships

Personal Needs + School Practices	How and Why Each Personal Need and School Practice Affect Relationships	Relationships
Voice + Equity		Recognition
Belonging + Community		Acceptance
Choice + Opportunity		Trust
Freedom + Responsibility		Respect
Imagination + Challenge		Purpose
Success + Expectations		Confirmation

Source: Personalize Learning, LLC.

Conversation Starters

- Which one of the personal needs is a concern for you in your classroom? Why?
- What school practice needs to be a priority at your school or district? Why?
- How can this activity help you better understand what it means to have a positive Culture of Learning?

BUILD A CULTURE OF LEARNING

What does **Culture of Learning** really mean? It can mean different things to different people. We created this comparison of the Culture of "one size fits all" with the culture of "learning." Figure 9.2 on the following page shows the common words or language that keep appearing in the conversations about these approaches to teaching and learning.

Personalized learning and the terms that represent learning can be confusing. Actually, it is all about semantics. Change the word *student* to *learner* and think about the teacher as a guide or facilitator of learning. Being a student implies that learning starts with the curriculum and is done to you. Being an expert learner means that learning is self-directed and can happen anywhere and anytime. As a partner in learning, the teacher is a co-designer and co-learner with his or her learners. Terms tend to get lost in translation because *personalized* means something different to different organizations.

Figure 9.2 Culture Comparison

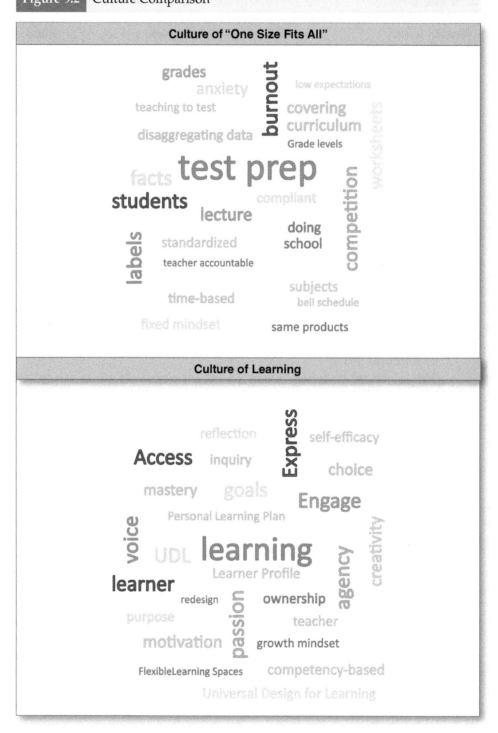

Source: Personalize Learning, LLC.

Consider that learning is "personal" when it starts with the learner rather than technology. A personalized learning environment is about the relationships and building a Culture of Learning.

Build a Strong Classroom Culture

Every school is unique and has its own demographics and issues. Every learner comes to school with his or her strengths, challenges, background, and concerns. In fact, each class is unique because of the teacher and how the teacher teaches and presents what it means to be part of the class. One way to build the culture is to start the year getting to know each other. The time you spend building a strong classroom culture in the first few weeks of school will pay returns every day of the year.

You can build a compassionate classroom and place relationships that are based on trust and respect at the center of the classroom. We recommend postponing any academics for the first two weeks and develop the relationships between you and your learners, starting with these:

- Invite each learner to create her or his Learner Profile.
- Consult with each learner and listen closely to his or her story so you can validate the child as a learner. This works really well if there is another adult in the room or a substitute so you have time with each learner.

Culture-Building Activities

You can use any of these culture- or team-building activities for learners to get to know and care about each other. Consider these activities to encourage learner voice and collaborative teamwork:

> **Pause/Think/Reflect**
>
> All of us are learners. We were born curious and open to learning or we wouldn't walk and talk. It's just how each of us was made. Learning is part of us. We were not born students—we were born learners. Our first experiences of learning were through play and discovery.

> **Consider This!**
>
> *Our first question should be, "What do children need?," followed immediately by "How can we meet those needs?"* Alfie Kohn

1. **Talents and Skills:** Have learners share talents and skills they have, no matter how small or large. Create a chart or collage for learners to add their talents using Post-it notes or writing on the chart. They can add as many Post-it notes as they want but make sure they add their names. You can use this list and invite learners to lead seminars about their talent or skill to other learners.

2. **Active Listening Strategy:**
   a. Pair learners and have them face each other.
   b. Have one person share about herself or himself for one minute. Have the other person really listen by looking into the speaker's eyes without saying anything or nodding her or his head.

     c. Then have the other person share with the partner, with the listener really listening.

     d. The pairs then share what they heard about the other person to another pair.

3. **Me Too Activity:** Have learners share something about themselves, such as "I like Minecraft." If other learners also like Minecraft, they stand up and say "Me too!" Continue to invite learners to share something and see who else has the same interests or facts. Then give them time to share with each other.

4. **Two Truths and a Lie:** You can create a circle or set up a forum or a Google Doc where learners can share two things that are true about themselves and one that is a lie. Then invite learners to try to guess which is the lie. They can then reply online or in the circle.

5. **What if?:** Pair learners and have them come up with a "What if" question to give the class. Then each pair leads a discussion. Example: "What if the British won the Revolutionary War?" Then have the pair that is leading invite others to come up with ideas about "What if _____ happened."

ACTIVITY 9.2
Culture-Building Activities

- Try one or two of these culture-building activities with your class or teachers in professional development.
- Share with another teacher how it worked, what worked well, and what you might try next time so learners can build trust and community with others.
- Go to the Companion Website and answer the Conversation Starters about culture building.

Conversation Starters

- How can you have the time at the beginning of the year to get to know each learner and build the culture?
- Share any other culture-building activities that you use with your learners.
- What challenges do you have with culture-building activities?
- How can you make this change in your classroom, school, or district?

Rich Czyz is director of curriculum and instruction at Stafford Township School District (pre-K through sixth grade) and Trevor Bryan, a K–5 art teacher in New Jersey, are co-founders of the Four O-Clock Faculty blog (fouroclockfaculty.com) that provides tips and tricks for educators and offered to share a few here in this section on culture.

Improve Classroom Culture

Rich Czyz and Trevor Bryan shared five ways to improve classroom culture that you can use with your classroom:

1. **Simplify rules in your classroom.** Many classrooms contain a list of rules that guide daily interactions. There is no list that can address every situation that may arise in the classroom, so think simply. Provide learners with a basic framework for your class expectations. Find something that works for you and gives learners a supportive structure that they can reference as they interact everyday. Rather than have a hard line of rules and consequences, these broad guiding principles provided flexibility in meeting the needs of all learners.

2. **Use the class meeting.** In my class, we held a class meeting once a week, or more often if necessary. Every Friday, we would clear our tables out of the way and put all the chairs in a giant circle. Then we would spend a half-hour sharing our successes as well as talking through problems or issues important to the class. It was important that students knew how to provide constructive criticism to classmates. This had to be explicitly modeled for learners. These conversations are so important to the well-being of the entire class—learners and teachers alike!

3. **Rethink consequences** from Trevor Bryan.

    If you do not do your work,

    1. I will sit with you.
    2. I will talk with you.
    3. I will listen to you.
    4. We will work together to figure out a plan so you can do your work.
    5. I will root for you like crazy.

4. **Honor choice and voice.** I offer multiple ways for learners to have a say in how and when they complete homework by using the "choose your own adventure" method. This gives learners the opportunity to choose which nights are best to complete assignments. Allow learners to demonstrate their learning using different learning modalities. Choice boards can be used to provide a variety of learning activities based on learner interest and need. A choice board can be set up on a 3x3 grid giving learners a choice between nine activities relating to the learning concept or unit of study.

5. **Treat everyone as a VIP (Very Important Person).** Use feedback to coach your learners by modeling what you would like to see in your

classroom. Check in with each learner and provide specific feedback to improve performance. Think ahead to support and meet the needs of all learners. Consider which learners may struggle during a lesson and provide multiple strategies to reduce barriers and maximize learning. Another thing to consider is using ARE (Appreciation Recognition Encouragement) to build up confidence and self-esteem among both individuals and teams that are performing exceptionally well. You can try a letter, thank you note, a positive word, or a pat on the back. You can even try a call home to a learner who showed kindness to another learner who was being picked on. By showing this type of appreciation to learners, you will build a positive classroom culture, while getting learners to invest in their own learning. (Czyz & Bryan, 2015)

www.personalizelearning
.com/2015/09/back-to-school-
with-four-oclock-faculty.html

Pause/Think/Reflect

Teachers: *How can you provide voice and choice in your class to build a Culture of Learning?*

Every learner needs to feel she or he is a valued member of the community—especially teenagers who need to be socially accepted by their peers. Learners want to have a voice but they need opportunities to share their opinions and ideas in an environment that encourages risk-taking and challenging thinking.

Pernille Ripp is a former fourth-, fifth-, and now seventh-grade teacher in Oregon, Wisconsin, who shared her own story about transforming learning in the last chapter. She explains thoughtful strategies for reflecting on how the culture changes in her book, *Passionate Learners* (2015). We are honored to share an excerpt from her book about these ideas teachers need to ask themselves.

Reflection Is Where We Begin

Pernille Ripp, seventh grade teacher in Oregon School District, Wisconsin, and author of Passionate Learners

Pernille Ripp, in her book *Passionate Learners* (2015), provides suggestions for how teachers how can make learning visible. The following bullets are excerpts from her book:

- **Look around your room.** What does it signal? Can learners move around freely or do you dictate it?
- **Film yourself teaching.** Are you talking more than your learners? Are they not listening and were you too focused on covering the curriculum?
- **Have learners time you.** Set the timer for 10 minutes and when it goes off, stop talking. If you need more time, negotiate with your learners.
- **Give them time to be experts.** Find out what your learners are passionate about. Then facilitate opportunities for them to share their expertise.
- **Stop answering all of their questions (or at least some of them).** Ask a question back instead of answering or refusing to answer. Ask something like "How will you find out?" and maybe keep going by asking, "How else can you find out?" Also wait and see if other learners share the answer or help another learner.
- **Have a frank conversation with your learners.** This is about admitting your own mistakes and maybe what you don't like about your teaching or the classroom. Then invite their opinions, withholding all judgment.
- **Be open to feedback.** If your learners are willing to share their honest opinions, then be open to listening to it without getting defensive. You can start the year off with a survey to find out their hopes, dreams, and fears.
- **Don't stop asking yourself the hard questions.** Would you still like being a learner in your classroom? Trust in yourself and your ability to create a better environment for all the learners who are in your class. Push yourself forward so that you do not become stuck in routine. Learners change every year and so should our approach.
- **Give it time.** Start with small changes. Remember progress is progress, no matter how small. (Ripp, 2015)

Pernille invites teachers to consider this question: "Would you want to be a learner in your class today? And if you are not sure, why don't you ask former or current learners how the whole year experience was for them."

ACTIVITY 9.3
Value Every Learner

For learners to grow and flourish, we need to create learning environments where every child is recognized as a learner. A culture that values every learner will empower learners to discover the joy of learning.

Collaborate with others in your school to answer these questions. How can you create a school culture that

- guides learners to think deeply about their learning?
- teaches them how to make sense of their learning?
- helps them set learning goals to support their learning?
- understands the tools, resources, and strategies each learner needs?
- assists learners in developing the skills to be independent and self-directed?
- nurtures their talents, interests, and aspirations so they can realize their hopes and dreams?

You can do Activity 9.3 at a staff meeting face-to-face or set up a Google doc to collaborate online.

Conversation Starters

Consider the culture in your own classroom. Some schools have underlying issues that no one wants to talk about. To change culture, all issues or problems need to be on the table. Go to the page Value Every Learner on the Companion Website to answer the following questions:

- What might be keeping you from changing the culture in your classroom? Keep all names private.
- What questions do you have for other teachers who might be in the same situation as you?

REDESIGN THE LEARNING ENVIRONMENT

The idea of creating environments that are learner-centered sounds attractive. However, developing a culture around learners and building systems to support learner-centered environments takes time and a process. Teachers find that when they want to change the culture and build relationships, a traditional classroom with desks in rows does not work.

Current Resources

When you redesign your learning environment, you will want to do an inventory of all the resources you have available for you and your learners. When learners take ownership of their learning, they choose and use the appropriate resources and tools they need to meet their learning goals and task. So knowing what is currently available will help you and your learners have multiple options for accessing resources. We've provided a sample inventory that you can download on the Companion Website.

Share the results of your inventory with your colleagues and your learners. You may find that you have resources that you do not use, but another teacher might have been wanting those resources for his or her classroom. After you fill out the inventory, then you want to determine where everything is in your classroom and your school. Now is the time to be objective and not get too close and personal with the "stuff" and "the way it is."

Review Your Learning Environment

Before you redesign your learning space, think about your class(es), their strengths, and the challenges of your learners. Consider these questions about your environment:

- When you walk into your room, what impressions do you get? Does it feel and look like your learners own it? Or do you drive it?
- Are you spending too much time setting up and adding to your classroom walls and materials?
- Do you need your desk? This is scary for some teachers but really think through why you need your desk and what is in it. Do you need all the stuff?
- How will you design new learning spaces to support all the learners in your class?
- How can you provide a flexible environment that encourages voice and choice?
- What new types of furniture might you need to add or replace?
- How are you using or underusing the spaces in your classroom?
- Do you have places for learners to pace, sit on the floor, use mobile devices, or have any quiet space for reflection?
- Can your learners use spaces outside the classroom such as the hall or outdoors?

ACTIVITY 9.4
Redesign the Learning Environment

Share how you would redesign your classroom in a reflection on the Companion Website.

1. Redesign your classroom using the *Designing Your Classroom* program (EdTech Leaders Online, n.d.) available on Companion Website, scan a drawing, or take pictures of your class to share with other teachers in your school or district.

2. Add a reflection on why you designed your classroom, office, library, or lab the way you did.

3. Reply thoughtfully to others about their designs and consider how you can apply some of their ideas to your design.

CONNECT THE DOTS

When you personalize learning, teacher and learner roles change. But something else happens: how you teach changes and then affects existing initiatives and programs. The issue we want to talk about here is that personalizing learning is not and should not be considered a new initiative that you add to your repertoire. Consider personalized learning to be the umbrella that connects the dots of all your initiatives and programs (Figure 9.3). Some people are concerned that the terms *personalized* and *personalization* are something that is done TO the learner.

If we change the concept so everything starts with the learner and you connect your programs, initiatives, and teaching strategies under the umbrella, it doesn't matter what you call it. It's the big picture of transforming teaching and learning so the focus is on the learner instead of the instruction, the curriculum, and the technology. Table 9.2 gives an example of one initiative, **Response to Intervention (RtI)** moving from a Culture of "one size fits all" to a Culture of Learning, **Response to Learning (RtL).**

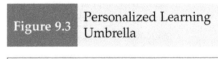
| Figure 9.3 | Personalized Learning Umbrella |

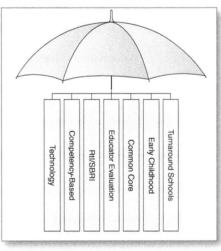

Source: Personalize Learning, LLC; Umbrella © TPopova/iStock Photos

Table 9.2   Example of Connecting Dots (RtI to RtL)

Culture of "One Size Fits All"	Culture of Learning
Response to Intervention (RtI)	**Response to Learning (RtL)**
We identify students at risk for poor learning outcomes, monitor learner progress, and provide and adjust interventions to identify students with learning disabilities or other disabilities. We view RtI as a way to qualify learners for special education, trying interventions before referring struggling students for traditional special education testing and placement. We also implement RtI from a compliance perspective, doing just enough to meet mandates, and have a desire to teach to the test to raise test scores.	Instead of waiting until a learner fails, we target each learner's specific learning needs when the learner needs it. That's why we will call it *Response to Learning*. In a personalized learning environment, learners own and drive learning by designing learning goals with their teacher. The teacher is a partner in learning as they both monitor progress on learning goals right from the beginning of the learning process. The teacher designs learning strategies identified through the Universal Design for Learning (UDL) lens so learning strategies can be identified earlier and as learners learn. Teachers and learners work together so learners receive additional support before they fail. Failure is no longer an option under a personalized learning environment.
Key Words: students, compliance, mandates, test scores, struggling, special education, at risk, poor learning outcomes, interventions, disabilities, teach to test	**Key Words:** learners, learning, ownership, driving learning, Universal Design for Learning, UDL, partners in learning, learning goals, failure no longer an option, personalized learning environment, assessment as they learn

Source: **Personalize Learning, LLC.**

ACTIVITY 9.5
Connect the Dots

If personalized learning is the umbrella to all the initiatives or programs in your school or district, then what does that mean for what you are mandated to implement? This is a 45-minute to 1-hour activity that you can do with your colleagues at your school or district.

You can do this activity with your entire staff with multiple groups where each group takes one initiative or program. Each group consists of five to six teachers and administrators.

1. Share the Culture Comparison keywords sample chart (Figure 9.2) and then have each group discuss what a Culture of Learning will mean at their schools or in their classrooms.

2. Demonstrate what moving from Culture of "one size fits all" to Culture of Learning with the example of RtI to RtL.

3. Ask each group to choose an initiative or program that members are either required to do or is built into the daily practice. Some examples of initiatives or programs that you can choose from that might change under the personalized learning umbrella:
   - English Language Learners, Technology Integration, Educator Effectiveness, Parent-Teacher Conferences, Assessment, Common Core, Professional Development, etc.

4. Use the Table 9.3 Connect the Dots template on the Companion Website or draw the chart on a flip chart to brainstorm how you will connect the dots.

5. Add the keywords for each section.

6. Have the groups share how they connected the initiative or program under the personalized learning umbrella.

Table 9.3   Connect the Dots Template

Culture of "One Size Fits All"	Culture of Learning
Key Words:	Key Words:

Source: Personalize Learning, LLC.

Conversation Starters

- How do you or did you move from a Culture of "one size fits all" to a Culture of Learning?
- How do we support teachers as they change their roles?
- Will the technology you chose support new teacher and learner roles?
- How will learners acquire the skills to choose and use the appropriate resources?

Let's assume you move to a Culture of Learning around the particular initiative or program you explored in the Connect the Dots activity. How has the culture changed in your school or district?

As the culture changes, teacher and learner roles change. Teachers need ongoing support to change how they teach and transform the culture in the classroom. Patrick Riley, a cognitive coach who works with teacher leaders in Kentucky, walks you through his coaching journey so you can experience what it is like to grow a Culture of Learning in classrooms.

Growing a Personalized Culture of Learning

By Patrick Riley

Throughout my coaching journey, the most powerful professional resource I can give teacher leaders is a safety net of support, in conjunction with school and district administration, for each teacher to grow and thrive at her or his own pace and level of commitment. My role is to encourage teacher leaders to take risks, to celebrate when they soar, and to catch them when they fall.

Ms. Jessica Morris's Burns Middle School science classroom was not for the pedagogical faint of heart. . . . Learners hustled with collaborative intent as they created prototypes for energy efficient model homes. Project partners huddled around iPad minis while experimenting with the thermodynamic properties of insulated cardboard houses. And, learners hummed with the collective, captivating buzz of curiosity in the self-paced pursuit of scientific insight. Alas, Ms. Morris's class possessed an electric alchemy that radiated a "Culture of Learning."

To be certain, this personalized Culture of Learning was not the traditional, typical environment marked by forerunners 20 years ago. The personalized learning strategies used in this classroom were not the methods taught to preservice teachers 10 years ago. In fact, it was not even the learning style that Ms. Morris herself employed as recently as 2 years ago. For Ms. Morris and her learners, the learning taking place in this seventh-grade classroom was an amalgamation of learner-centered, curiosity-provoking activities, galvanized in the fires of learner passions that transcended even the most stubborn traces of teenage apathy.

In essence, this learner-centered environment was the maturation, the development of one tiny seed planted in the fall of 2014. Read more about the seed of personalized learning on our website. (Riley, 2016)

Patrick Riley is a cognitive coach, Green River Regional Educational Cooperative, kid·FRIENDLy, Race to the Top-District Grant in Kentucky. Patrick works closely with more than 30 Kentucky teacher leaders (working in 10 schools and 3 school districts) to embed person-

www.personalizelearning .com/2016/01/growing-personalized-culture-of-learning. html

alized learning strategies in the classroom, helping teachers further inspire, challenge, empower, and engage learners through the constructive process of learning.

CREATE A RATIONALE TO PERSONALIZE LEARNING

Changing the way you teach and how learners learn is a shift by growing a Culture of Learning. You may get questions about why you are making these changes in your class. How will you introduce the idea of growing a Culture of Learning to your class and other teachers? What if a parent or fellow teacher asks you, "Why would you personalize learning?" What would you say? The idea of creating a 60-second speech is to have something ready—either a speech, poem, song, video, animation, or presentation. A 60-second speech is about 100 to 150 words. What is an elevator pitch? If you haven't heard the term, it doesn't mean you've never given one. It's basically a challenge to sell your idea, a new product or service, or even yourself, in the time it takes for the elevator to travel several floors. We included several 60-second speeches in different forms on the Companion Website as ideas for you.

ACTIVITY 9.6
60-Second Elevator Speech

The attention span of the average person is just 30 seconds before his or her mind starts wandering. Another reason to create a short speech is that people have less time today. You need to grab them quickly or you may lose them.

1. Brainstorm and plan ideas around what you came up with your common language for personalized learning.

2. Find language that everyone understands. Don't use acronyms or educational jargon.

3. Use words that are powerful and strong to grab their attention.

4. Include words that create a visual image in your listener's mind. This will make your message memorable.

5. Start with a "hook" that snags your listener's interest and makes them want to know more. This is the phrase or words that strike a chord in your listeners.

Conversation Starters

Check out the example 60-second elevator speeches on the Companion Website.

- Why do you need a rationale to personalize learning?
- What is the best format to get your point across?
- How will you hook your audience?

This chapter is for you to rethink what the Culture of Learning is all about. We share what you can do to help learners take more responsibility for their learning. You can be the change and part of the process to transform teaching and learning one step at a time.

Build the Common Language

Add the common language to the list that you started from the previous chapters.

- Update your common language in the Padlet after what you learned about building relationships, redesigning the learning environment, and connecting the dots under the personalized learning umbrella.
- At this point, you have now compiled the common language from each chapter. Consider conducting an activity to see how words in the common language are connected to each other and where the patterns may be.

- Go back and review your vision and shared beliefs from Chapter 1 and decide how you may want to incorporate the common language there.

Review: Collect all the activities you did and keep this practical guide close as you go through the exciting journey of personalizing learning.

Learn: Keep coming back to this guide and the Companion Website to start the conversations about your own journey.

Apply: Keep a journal or post on your own blog or website. Let us know how your journey is growing a Culture of Learning and how your learners developed their voice in the process.

We hope you found this guide helpful
for you on your journey to personalize learning

You can take small steps each day to move to learner-centered environments. Consider some of the ideas from this book that you can use right away. Write down any questions you still have and use the Conversation Starters on the Companion Website to ask us and other readers of this book any questions you may have about personalized learning. We hope the stories in this book give you pictures of what personalized learning looks like and the activities help you frame how to personalize learning. We created this practical guide to be there for you as you dip your toes or just dive right into personalized learning environments. Keep it with you to grab ideas when you have questions, need an activity, design a lesson or a project, or are looking for a story to share. As you change how you teach, your learners will change how they learn. Share your "Wow" stories.

This is going to be an exciting journey for you and your learners, so have fun and enjoy the learning that happens. We look forward to learning more about you, and all of us can be on this journey together to personalize learning for all learners. Thank you so much for reading our book and sharing the journey with us.

—Barbara and Kathleen

Glossary

Access: How a learner first processes information by accessing content through digital media, visual media, printed text, audio means, or touch.

Agency: The capacity of individuals to act independently and to make their own free choices.

Assessment AS Learning: Assessment characterized by learners reflecting on their own learning and making adjustments so they achieve deeper understanding.

Assessment FOR Learning: Assessment designed to make each learner's understanding visible so that teachers can decide what they can do to help learners progress. (Formative)

Assessment OF Learning: Assessment that typically comes at the end of a course or unit of instruction to determine the extent to which instructional goals have been achieved. (Summative)

Blended Learning: Hybrid learning that combines online and on-site opportunities.

Class Learning Snapshot™ (CLS): Helps teachers universally design lessons based on looking at the extremes of four diverse learners in their classes instead of on the average learner.

Class Learning Toolkit™ (CLT): Helps teachers plan for the materials and methods that all learners in their classes can use during their lessons and units by referring to the CLS.

Competency-Based: Refers to any system of academic instruction, assessment, grading, and reporting that is based on learners demonstrating mastery of the knowledge and skills they are expected to learn before they progress to the next lesson, get promoted to the next grade level, or receive a diploma. This can also be called performance-based or proficiency-based.

Culture of Learning: When the people in a school community build the common language around learners first. The focus is on building relationships between teachers and learners so everyone has a sense of belonging and caring for each other to meet everyone's fullest potential.

Engage: How each learner engages with content and concepts using multiple strategies and tools that will keep the learner's interest and motivation to learn.

Expert Learner: The expert learner develops learning goals so she or he can acquire the necessary skills to become an independent and self-directed learner. Expert learners understand their strengths and challenges and how to navigate their learning environments, where to seek out resources, and who to connect with to collaborate and consult with in any learning situation.

Express: How each learner expresses what he or she knows and understands through actions, that is, through writing, acting, presenting, building, drawing, sharing, and so forth.

Extended Learning Opportunities: Also known as ELOs, where learners are paired with mentors in a work or business environment where learners gain insight and experiences in a field they may be interested in. Some schools offer programs where learners design their own pathways to graduation. In these programs, learners can practice as apprentices or take online high school or college courses. Each of these experiences will prepare the learner to be future ready for college, career, and life.

Flow: When a person is fully immersed in what she or he is doing and there is a balance between the challenge of the task and the skill of the learner.

Learner Portfolio: Where the learner demonstrates evidence of learning along with his or her reflection so the learner has a record of her or his achievements.

Learner Profile™ (LP): Identifies how learners learn best based on how they access information, engage with content, and express what they know. The LP also addresses their strengths, challenges, interests, aspirations, talents, and passions.

Learning Goals: Goals derived from a learner's Learner Profile and Personal Learning Backpack that are focused on developing independent learning skills to support the learner's own learning.

Lexile Score: Refers to a measurement and tracking of reading abilities that helps teachers choose appropriate reading materials based on the learner's abilities.

Mindset: Belief guides a large part of a person's life. He or she can have either a fixed or a growth mindset. Much of what someone thinks of as his or her personality actually grows out of this mindset. A fixed mindset can prevent anyone from fulfilling his or her potential. A growth mindset is when someone believes that he or she can do accomplish something if the effort is put in.

Motivation: Motivation has a great impact on the learning process. Some people learn more by outside influences, but others may achieve more by engaging in what is personally rewarding for its own sake (intrinsic motivation) rather than the desire for some external reward (extrinsic motivation).

Neuroscience: Links observations about cognitive behavior with the actual physical processes that support such behavior.

Orton-Gillingham: The Orton-Gillingham approach to reading instruction was developed in the early 20th century. This intensive, sequential, multisensory, phonics-based system teaches the basics of word formation before whole meanings. Research has indicated this system is effective in remediating instruction for students with dyslexia.

Personal Learning Backpack™ (PLB): The PLB is personal to the learner based on how the learner understands how he or she learns best and includes learning strategies and skills, resources, apps, and tools.

Personal Learning Plan™ (PLP): The PLP has four areas of focus with related goals to prepare the learner to be independent, self-directed, and future ready: Access, Engage, and Express Goals for skill development; Personal Goals; College and Career Goals; and Citizenship Goals. Each goal in the PLP is designed with the learner so the learner develops agency.

Project-Based Learning (PBL): Dynamic approach to teaching in which learners explore real-world problems and challenges. PBL is not the same as learners all doing the same project designed by the teacher.

Response to Intervention (RtI): A multitier approach to the early identification and support of students with learning and behavior needs (see www.rtinetwork.org).

Response to Learning (RtL): An approach that allows learners to monitor their progress and adjust learning and for teachers to provide support as learners are learning.

School Culture: "Refers to the beliefs, perceptions, relationships, attitudes, and written and unwritten rules that shape and influence every aspect of how a school functions, but the term also encompasses more concrete issues such as the physical and emotional safety of students, the orderliness of classrooms and public spaces, or the degree to which a school embraces and celebrates racial, ethnic, linguistic, or cultural diversity." (http://edglossary.org/school-culture/)

Self-Efficacy: Learners with a strong sense of self-efficacy approach complex and challenging learning tasks with a sense of confidence that if they use good strategies, practice smart persistence, and use the full range of resources available to them, they can and will succeed (Wigfield & Wagner, 2005).

Shared Beliefs: A foundation of shared beliefs about learners, teachers, and learning communities needs to be established by all the stakeholders in the community. Each community needs to know and understand what they value in the education of their children.

Stage One PLE: Teacher universally designs instruction that encourages learner voice and choice.

Stage Two PLE: Learner and teacher are co-designers of lessons, projects, and assessments.

Stage Three PLE: Learner drives her or his learning with teacher as partner in learning.

Universal Design for Learning (UDL): Set of principles for curriculum development that gives all individuals equal opportunities to learn.

UDL Guidelines: The nine UDL Guidelines are organized around the three UDL Principles. The UDL Guidelines serve as a framework for teachers to use in choosing tools, methods, and practices in planning universally designed lessons that can reduce barriers to learning as well as maximizing learning for all learners.

UDL Principles: The UDL Principles can serve as a lens for teachers to use to understand how learners learn best and for learners to understand how they learn. These principles include multiple means of representation (how learners need to *access* information), multiple means of engagement (how learners need to *engage* with the content), and multiple means of action and expression (how learners need to *express* what they know and understand.)

Variability: Refers to the infinite range of combinations that make up learners. (National Center on Universal Design for Learning, 2014)

Vision: If a school or district wants to move forward, it needs to develop an understood, agreed-on vision with all stakeholders. It is important to identify where the school or district wants to go in relation to where they are as the key to understand the areas needed for improvement.

References and
Additional Resources

Bandura, A. (1986). *Social foundations of thought and action: A social cognitive theory.* Englewood Cliffs, NJ: Prentice Hall.

Bandura, A. (1991, February). Human agency: The rhetoric and the reality. *American Psychologist, 46,* 156–161.

Block, J. (2014, October 30). *Student choice leads to student voice.* Retrieved February 4, 2016, from http://www.edutopia.org/blog/student-choice-leads-to-voice-joshua-block

Bray, B. (2013, July 14). *Responsibility vs. accountability.* Retrieved October 13, 2015, from http://www.personalizelearning.com/2013/07/responsibility-vs-accountability.html

Bray, B. (2015, October 28). *Learner voice demonstrates commitment to agency.* Retrieved June 21, 2016, from http://www.personalizelearning.com/2015/10/learner-voice-demonstrates-commitment.html

Bray, B., & McClaskey, K. (2014, June 25). *Updated personalization vs. differentiation vs. individualization chart version 3.* Retrieved January 12, 2016, from http://www.personalizelearning.com/2013/03/new-personalization-vs-differentiation.html

Bray, B., & McClaskey, K. (2014, December 14). *Access, engage, and express: The lens for teaching and learning.* Retrieved January 10, 2016, from http://www.personalizelearning.com/2014/12/access-engage-and-express-lens-for.html

Bray, B., & McClaskey, K. (2015). *Make learning personal: The what, who, wow, where, and why.* Thousand Oaks, CA: Corwin.

Bray, B., & McClaskey, K. (S. Duckworth, illustrator). (2015, November 8). *Continuum of choice: Choice is more than a menu of options.* Retrieved December 11, 2015, from http://www.personalizelearning.com/2015/11/choice-is-more-than-menu-of-options.html

Bray, B., & McClaskey, K. (S. Duckworth, illustrator). (2016, January 10). *Continuum of voice: What it means for the learner.* Retrieved February 1, 2016, from http://www.personalizelearning.com/2016/01/continuum-of-voice-what-it-means-for.html

Bray, B., & McClaskey, K. (2016, February 14). *New version: Stages of personalized learning environments* (v5). Retrieved May 25, 2016, from http://www.personalizelearning.com/2016/02/new-version-stages-of-personalized.html

Bray, B., & McClaskey, K. (S. Duckworth, illustrator). (2016, March 6). *Continuum of engagement: From compliant to flow*. Retrieved March 10, 2016, from http://www.personalizelearning.com/2016/03/continuum-of-engagement.html

Bray, B., & McClaskey, K. (S. Duckworth, illustrator). (2016, March 22). *Continuum of motivation: Moving from extrinsic to intrinsic motivation*. Retrieved March 26, 2016, from http://www.personalizelearning.com/2016/03/continuum-of-motivation-moving-from.html

Bray, B., & McClaskey, K. (S. Duckworth, illustrator). (2016, April 17). *Continuum of ownership: Developing autonomy*. Retrieved April 19, 2016, from http://www.personalizelearning.com/2016/04/continuum-of-ownership-developing.html

Bray, B., & McClaskey, K. (S. Duckworth, illustrator). (2016, May 9). *Continuum of self-efficacy: Path to perseverance*. Retrieved June 21, 2016, from http://www.personalizelearning.com/2016/05/continuum-of-self-efficacy-path-to.html

Bray, B., & McClaskey, K. (S. Duckworth, illustrator). (2016, June 5). *Continuum of purpose: Fostering a meaningful life*. Retrieved June 21, 2016, from http://www.personalizelearning.com/2016/06/continuum-of-purpose-fostering.html

Buck Institute for Education (BIE). (n.d.). *Planning forms*. Retrieved January 12, 2016, from http://bie.org/objects/cat/planning_forms

Cherry, K. (2016, January 15). *Extrinsic vs. intrinsic motivation: What's the difference?* Retrieved January 25, 2016, from http://psychology.about.com/od/motivation/f/difference-between-extrinsic-and-intrinsic-motivation.htm

Clarke, J., & Frazer, E. (2003). Making learning personal: Educational practices that work. In J. DiMartino, J. Clarke, & D. Wolk (Eds.), *Personalized learning: Preparing high school students to create their futures* (pp. 174–193). Lanham, MD: Scarecrow Press.

Csikszentmihalyi, M. (1990). *Flow: The psychology of optimal experience*. New York, NY: Harper & Row.

Csikszentmihalyi, M. (2016). *Mihaly Csikszentmihalyi*. Retrieved February 1, 2016, from http://www.pursuit-of-happiness.org/history-of-happiness/mihaly-csikszentmihalyi/

Czyz, R. (2015, September 3). *Back to school with Four O'Clock Faculty*. Retrieved January 12, 2016, from http://www.personalizelearning.com/2015/09/back-to-school-with-four-oclock-faculty.html

Czyz, R., & Bryan, T. (2015, October 12). *5 ways to improve classroom culture*. Retrieved February 2, 2016, from http://fouroclockfaculty.com/2015/10/5-ways-to-improve-classroom-culture/

Dake, RJ. 2008. Driving Questions: Retrieved June 10, 2016, from http://www.jetspost.com/eportfolio/pbl/driving_questions.htm

EdTech Leaders Online. (n.d.). *Designing your classroom*. Retrieved March 1, 2016, from http://courses.edtechleaders.org/html_cores/trainingcores/multimedia/classroom_app/

The Education Alliance at Brown University. (2016). *Teaching diverse learners*. Retrieved March 11, 2016, from https://www.brown.edu/academics/education-alliance/teaching-diverse-learners/

Ford, P. (2016, March 3). *Personalize learning: Project-based learning gives kindergarteners agency*. Retrieved March 10, 2016, from http://www.personalizelearning.com/2016/03/project-based-learning-gives.html

Fredricks, J. A., Blumenfeld, P. C., & Paris, A. H. (2004). School engagement: Potential of the concept, state of the evidence. *Review of Educational Research*, 74(1), 59–109.

Gerstein, J., (2015, August 9). *Today's education should be about giving learners voice and choice*. Retrieved November 13, 2015, from https://usergeneratededucation. wordpress.com/2015/08/09/todays-education-should-be-about-giving-learners-voice-and-choice/

Hammonds, V. (2015, December 15). *Personalize learning: It takes a village to personalize learning in Maine and in Oz*. Retrieved January 20, 2016, from http://www.personalizelearning.com/2015/12/it-takes-village-to-personalize.html

Hinckley, E. (2015, May). *I like, I wish, I wonder: The power of feedback*. Retrieved April 6, 2016, from http://21cm.org/21cm-u/learning/in-the-field/2015/05/12/i-like-i-wish-i-wonder-the-power-of-feedback/

How to craft a killer 60 second elevator pitch that will land you employment. (2016). Retrieved February 8, 2016, from http://www.salisbury.edu/careerservices/students/Interviews/60secondElevator.html

Jobs for the Future & the Council of Chief State School Officers. 2015. *Educator competencies for personalized, learner-centered teaching*. Boston, MA: Jobs for the Future.

Johnson, B. (2012, March 1). *How do we know when students are engaged?* Retrieved December 12, 2015, from http://www.edutopia.org/blog/student-engagement-definition-ben-johnson

Kaufman, S. B. (2014, March 5). *Interest fuels effortless engagement*. Retrieved December 13, 2015, from http://blogs.scientificamerican.com/beautiful-minds/interest-fuels-effortless-engagement/

Kouzes, J. M., & Posner, B. Z. (2008). *The leadership challenge* (4th ed.). San Francisco, CA: Jossey-Bass.

Klem, A. M., & Connell, J. P. (2004, September 1). Relationships matter: Linking teacher support to student engagement and achievement. *Journal of School Health, 74*(7), 262–273.

Maraboli, S. (n.d.). A quote from *Life, the truth, and being free*. Retrieved March 6, 2016, from http://www.goodreads.com/quotes/319514-as-for-the-journey-of-life-at-some-point-you

Martin-Kniep, G. (2012). *Neuroscience of engagement and SCARF: Why they matter to schools*. Retrieved March 2, 2016, from http://www.lciltd.org/files/NS of Engagement and SCARF_US.pdf

Maryland Learning Links. (2015, November 24). UDL case study: Instructional methods. Retrieved January 12, 2016, from https://marylandlearninglinks .org/resource/instructional-methods/

Mayer, A. (2015). *The difference between projects and project-based learning*. Retrieved November 23, 2015, from http://www.friedtechnology.com/#!stuff/c243p

McClaskey, K., (2014, November 14). *Changing perceptions—Every child a learner*. Retrieved November 12, 2015, from http://www.personalizelearning. com/2014/11/changing-perceptions-every-child-learner.html

McClaskey, K. (2015, October 15). *Discover the learner in every child*. Retrieved December 9, 2015, from http://www.personalizelearning.com/2015/10/discover-learner-in-every-child.html

McCombs, B. (2012). *Developing responsible and autonomous learners: A key to motivating students: Teachers' modules*. Washington, DC: American Psychological Association. Retrieved from http://www.apa.org/education/k12/learners.aspx

McGrath, W. (2015, July 3). *Personalize learning: Where are all the expert learners?* Retrieved November 2, 2015, from http://www.personalizelearning .com/2015/07/where-are-all-expert-learners.html

Meyer, A., Rose, D. H., & Gordon, D. (2014). Expert learning. In *Universal design for learning: Theory and practice* (pp. 21–48). Wakefield, MA: CAST Professional Publishing. Retrieved November 11, 2015, from http://udltheorypractice. cast.org/home?6

Meyer, A., Rose, D. H., & Gordon, D. (2014). *Universal design for learning: Theory and practice.* Wakefield, MA: CAST Professional Publishing.

Miller, A. (2015, September 22). *6 strategies to truly personalize PBL.* Retrieved January 12, 2016, from http://www.edutopia.org/blog/6-strategies-truly-personalize-pbl-andrew-miller

Miller, A. K. (2015). *Freedom to fail: How do I foster risk-taking and innovation in my classroom?* Alexandria, VA: ASCD.

National Center on Universal Design for Learning. (2014, July 31). *UDL and expert learners.* Retrieved November 7, 2015, from http://www.udlcenter.org/aboutudl/expertlearners

National Center on Universal Design for Learning. (2014, November 12). *UDL guidelines: Theory & practice version.* Retrieved November 8, 2015, from http://www.udlcenter.org/aboutudl/udlguidelines_theorypractice

Rickabaugh, J. (2015, September 28). *Self-efficacy: The secret sauce to learning success.* Retrieved January 14, 2016, from https://cesa1transformation.wordpress.com/2015/09/28/self-efficacy-the-secret-sauce-to-learning-success/

Rickabaugh, J. (2016). *Tapping the power of personalized learning: A roadmap for school leaders.* Alexandria, VA: ASCD.

Riley, P. (2016, January 31). *Personalize learning: Growing a personalized culture of learning.* Retrieved February 5, 2016, from http://www.personalizelearning.com/2016/01/growing-personalized-culture-of-learning.html

Ripp, P. (2015). *Passionate learners: How to engage and empower your students* (2nd ed., Eye on Education). London, England: Routledge.

Ripp, P. (2016, January 24). *Personalize learning: My transformation as a teacher.* Retrieved January 31, 2016, from http://www.personalizelearning.com/2016/01/my-transformation-as-teacher.html

Rose, D., & Gravel, J. (2012). Curricular opportunities in the digital age. *Students at the Center.* Retrieved February 5, 2016, from Students at the Center Web site: http://www.studentsatthecenter.org/topics/curricular-opportunities-digital-age

Rose, T. (2013, June 19). *The myth of average: Todd Rose TEDxSonomaCounty.* Retrieved November 11, 2015 from Tedx Talks website: http://youtu.be/4eBmyttcfU4

Sackstein, S. (2016, January 8). *Personalize learning: Putting the power of questions in the learner's hands.* Retrieved January 23, 2016, from http://www.personalizelearning.com/2016/01/putting-power-of-questions-in-learners.html

Sackstein, S. (2016). *The power of questioning: Opening up the world of student inquiry.* Lanham, MD: Rowman & Littlefield.

Schmitz, M., & Maynor, S. (2015, February 12). *Personalize learning: Discover EPiC—Re-imagine education.* Retrieved January 15, 2016, from http://www.personalizelearning.com/2015/02/discover-epic-re-imagine-education.html

Speck, M., & Stollenwerk, D. A. (1999). *The principalship: Building a learning community.* Upper Saddle River, NJ: Merrill.

Taylor, M. D. (1976). *Roll of thunder, hear my cry.* New York, NY: Dial Press.

Tomorrow Entertainment (Producer) & Smight, J. (Director). (1978). *Roll of Thunder Hear My Cry* [Motion picture]. United States: Artisan Entertainment. Retrieved March 1, 2016, from https://youtu.be/U2ZbrNMQtfo

Toshalis, E., & Nakkula, M. J. (2012). *Motivation, engagement, and student voice*. Retrieved November 15, 2015, from http://www.studentsatthecenter.org/topics/motivation-engagement-and-student-voice

Watkins, C. (2003). *Learning: A sense-maker's guide* (Professional Development Series). London, England: ATL. Retrieved February 12, 2016, from http://chriswatkins.net

Watkins, C. (2009). Learners in the driving seat. *School Leadership Today, 1*(2), 28–31. Retrieved January 15, 2016, from http://chriswatkins.net/wp-content/uploads/2015/07/Watkins-09-4-lnr-driven-SLT.pdf

Wigfield, A., & Wagner, A. L. (2005). Competence and motivation during adolescence. In A. J. Elliot & C. S. Dweck (Eds.), *Handbook of competence and motivation* (pp. 222–239). New York, NY: Guilford Press.

Index

A SAGE Publishing Company

CORWIN HAS ONE MISSION: to enhance education through intentional professional learning.

We build long-term relationships with our authors, educators, clients, and associations who partner with us to develop and continuously improve the best evidence-based practices that establish and support lifelong learning.

Solutions you want. Experts you trust. Results you need.

A UTHOR CONSULTING

Author Consulting

On-site professional learning with sustainable results! Let us help you design a professional learning plan to meet the unique needs of your school or district. www.corwin.com/pd

I NSTITUTES

Institutes

Corwin Institutes provide collaborative learning experiences that equip your team with tools and action plans ready for immediate implementation. www.corwin.com/institutes

E COURSES

eCourses

Practical, flexible online professional learning designed to let you go at your own pace. www.corwin.com/ecourses

R EAD2EARN

Read2Earn

Did you know you can earn graduate credit for reading this book? Find out how: www.corwin.com/read2earn

Contact an account manager at (800) 831-6640 or visit **www.corwin.com** for more information.

CPSIA information can be obtained
at www.ICGtesting.com
Printed in the USA
LVHW021003090422
715666LV00004B/70